A PROCESS APPROACH TO SUICIDE PREVENTION BEHIND BARS

A PROCESS APPROACH TO SUICIDE PREVENTION BEHIND BARS

✦

A Working Guide for Program Directors and Practitioners

Ronald L. Bonner, Psy.D.

iUniverse, Inc.
New York Lincoln Shanghai

A PROCESS APPROACH TO SUICIDE PREVENTION BEHIND BARS

A Working Guide for Program Directors and Practitioners

iUniverse books may be ordered through booksellers or by contacting:

iUniverse
2021 Pine Lake Road, Suite 100
Lincoln, NE 68512
www.iuniverse.com
1-800-Authors (1-800-288-4677)

This book does not offer formal training for developing or implementing a comprehensive suicide prevention program in correctional facilities. Expert advice, training, and consultation should be sought from competent professionals for these areas.

ISBN-13: 978-0-595-36982-9 (pbk)
ISBN-13: 978-0-595-81389-6 (ebk)
ISBN-10: 0-595-36982-0 (pbk)
ISBN-10: 0-595-81389-5 (ebk)

Printed in the United States of America

To my rowdy boys, Jason and Joshua, who provide more positive energy, reasons for living, and exhaustion than an old man can sometimes stand. May your lives grow in goodness and may you bring hope to those who are hurting and in darkness.

Noel, please continue to intercede on behalf of Jason and Joshua that their lives are always protected and guided by the Loving One you so faithfully served.

The degree of civilization in a society can be judged by entering its prisons.
—*Fyodor Dostoevsky*

I was in prison and you came to visit me. I assure you, when you did it to one of the least of these my brothers and sisters; you were doing it to me!
—*Jesus Christ*

Contents

Acknowledgments

The ideas in this work are credited to a number of wonderful individuals in my life who have provided friendship, companionship, and leadership along the way. By far, Lindsay Hayes has been the most influential leader in correctional suicide prevention. He was there for me nineteen years ago when I turned my preoccupation with suicide to a career in corrections, and he is still here today. I consider Lindsay to be the "Father of Correctional Suicidology," for he has a relentless passion for inmate suicide prevention and represents all that is good about correctional health care and human compassion. For the past, present, and future of clinical suicidology, Dr. Edwin S. Shneidman stands above all others in giving us the heart and soul of the "relationship work," that which ultimately makes psychache bearable and amenable to healing.

I also want to thank my mentor, Dr. Alex Rich, who has been my supporter and research partner for more than twenty years. We have done well. Special thanks go to Dr. Aylene Harper for getting me started in psychology. In one way or another, whatever good has come from my relationship work goes back to you. To my dear friend, teacher, and healer, the late Sr. Noel Mattes, O.S.F.: You have always represented the gospel life well-lived by so lovingly serving the needs of others. I still hear your voice so gently reminding me that taking care of those who are hurting is a miraculous privilege that touches the very Heart of the Suffering One. I regret the many times I have not listened and when my selfishness has gotten in the way of the work. Please keep praying for me.

I am blessed to have had a wonderful sister and brother-in-law, Judith and Austin Mallozzi, who raised me after the untimely death of my mother and during my father's endless battle with depression and the dark journey. I would not be where I am if it were not for your love and guidance. I am so thankful to the following individuals for touching my life and helping me realize what matters most in living: Fred Bercik (my ever so faithful friend), Mary Hamilton, Fr. Gus Milon, George Walter, the late Sr. Gus Taurish, St. Mother Theresa, Fr. Harold Parsons, Dennis Fall, Dr. Jim Davison, Pastor Doug Schader, Denielle Thomas, Lisa Edinger, and Dennis Hammond. My respect and appreciation are expressed to the outstanding "jailbird leaders," the late Dr. Al Smith, Warden G. C. Wigen, Warden Mike Zenk, Associate Warden Tom Szulanczyk, Associate Warden P. F. Ackley, and Associate Warden M. J. Fedorowicz. You ran outstanding jails, managed by walking and talking. You treated others on both sides of the fence with respect, and you tried your best to support the wisdom that a lower segregation count equates to a better jail. My deepest gratitude goes out to the love of my life, Diane, who has been the steady light tower of our family and managed to tolerate my obsessions with the dark journey and some of life's demons. We, in union with our Creator, have achieved our greatest blessings, Jason and Joshua. It is to them that this work is dedicated. Finally, to the many suicidal people behind bars that have allowed me to enter their worlds and painfully understand why the process of suicide makes experiential sense, you have been my best teachers and I hope our work has brought you lasting hope and reasons for living. For Urbano and Robert, who I lost along the way, I am so deeply sorry and pray you have found peace.

Introduction

The problem of suicide in jails, prisons, and juvenile detention facilities has garnered growing attention in recent years. Much work has been accomplished in identifying risk factors, constructing risk profiles, and developing effective prevention and intervention methods. Nevertheless, the field has generally remained static and piecemeal, bereft of an organizing framework to guide research, assessment, and intervention. A process model of suicide, as adapted from the general clinical suicidology literature, is proposed to provide such a framework and integrate the various core areas of inmate suicide prevention.

In this pursuit, this work will examine the incidence of correctional suicide, the stages of the suicide process, multimodal risk factors, screening and assessment, interventions, prevention programs, professional standards, risk management, and staff care. The following concepts are a culmination of literature review and the author's research and clinical experience in working with suicidal inmates over the past nineteen years. While these ideas may prove useful in guiding correctional and mental health care staff in developing and implementing programs, they are *not* a substitute for sound clinical assessment and intervention, which varies uniquely according to the stage and multimodal makeup of each suicidal inmate. Advanced suicide prevention training, consultation with experts in the field, and the exploitation of a number of available program resources are all strongly encouraged in this process. Fortunately, the field has advanced so appreciably that advice, guidance, professional guidelines, and research are all but a phone call or computer click away.

1

How I Got to Suicide behind Bars

A recent editorial evaluation of an earlier draft of this manuscript suggested I overwhelmed the reader with too much "dry stuff" and should instead personalize the material by describing some real-life experiences in my work with suicidal offenders. For those of you who work in corrections, your sense of system paranoia might tell you why I'm somewhat hesitant to get into too much case detail. However, I *will* share some personal experiences that have led me to the study of suicide behind bars; now a passion, but certainly never part of my career planning or aspirations.

Suicide has been on my mind since childhood. My mother died a terrible death of bone cancer when I was just four years old. I grew up with my father, a bright, caring, and successful man who nevertheless couldn't escape the biological curse of mental anguish. He endured serious bouts of depression and suicidal twinges throughout his adult life and was hospitalized many times and treated with numerous medications. Sadly, he improved only after undergoing regimens of electroconvulsive therapy. As he aged, his depression worsened and eventually seemed to destroy him. In his final days, he was inappropriately prescribed a large mixture of psychotropic medications—at his disposal. His death certificate noted the cause as Mycardio Infarction. I've never been able to stop wondering...

Soon after starting college, I knew I wanted to be a psychologist. I found abnormal psychology particularly intriguing, especially as it related to mood disorders and suicide. I searched for answers as to why some depressions and emotional pains do not improve with treatment. What was it about my father's curse that would not let go of his psyche? What causes a person to give up and simply want to die?

I ultimately came to understand the process a bit better while working as an undergraduate at a community mental health center and university medical center psychiatric institute. There I dealt with people who suffered seemingly unbearable mental anguish—people who saw suicide as perhaps the only alternative escape from the pain. When I went to graduate school, I quickly met up with a clinical professor whose research interests paralleled my own. We embarked on a very active research program on the cognitive, interpersonal, and life stress factors associated with depression and suicidal thoughts in college students. I was shocked to learn how many young college students in the prime of their lives suffer from depression and serious thoughts of suicide. My mind often drifted back to my father and I wondered if he too suffered so early in life.

In addition to a number of research studies, I worked clinically with depression and suicidality in college students from two university counseling centers, as well as inmates in a local jail and clients in a drug and alcohol treatment agency. In almost all studies and cases, suicide was seldom an isolated event. It was generally a process of stages that developed out of a person's inability to cope with seemingly insurmountable stressors and problems of living. Depression would develop, hopelessness would set in, psychache would take over, and suicide was typically seen as the only way out of a horribly painful existence.

After graduating and passing my licensure boards, I took a job as a staff psychologist at an inpatient crisis stabilization unit for inmates from a large county jail system. It was there that my preoccupation with suicide moved behind bars. I was shocked to learn that jail inmates were nine times more likely to commit suicide than members of the general population. The profile was very disheartening yet one that could apply to many of us at a certain point of our lives. Most jailed suicide victims were first time-offenders, intoxicated and arrested for an alcohol or drug-related offense such as a DUI. Most had no history of violence, and the majority had killed themselves in isolation during their first twenty-four hours of incarceration.

From there, I took a job as a psychologist at a maximum-security prison near the university where my fiancée (now wife) was completing her doctoral studies. I fully blame her for getting me in prison. I learned that the prisoners killed themselves less often than jail detainees but still at a high rate and usually in part for different reasons, such as problems in population, mental illness, victimization, and segregation placement.

While certainly not planned in advance or even initially considered, I have now worked with probably more than 1,000 suicidal inmates in a variety of correctional facilities. It has been a long and difficult nineteen years, mostly related not to inmates but to what I call "system nonsense," compulsive ego-masturbation, and a lot of pathetic "Little Peters" over-compensating and trying to emulate "Big Peters." The work with the suicidal offender, on the other hand, has alternately been rewarding and depressing and almost always anxiety provoking.

In nearly every case, as the thesis of this book suggests, there is a process by which a vulnerable offender, under highly stressful conditions of confinement and problematic day-to-day living, approaches a point of intolerable emotional pain and consequently contemplates or decides to end his or her life. I have often found the "life trigger" to be a relationship breakup, victimization, or conflict within the prison population, but there's almost always a major life problem pushing the inmate to the breaking point. There is often an underlying mental illness, such as major depression or bipolar disorder. And almost all the crisis calls I've fielded over the years have been in regard to inmates housed in segregation, under conditions of sensory deprivation and isolation. They are typically panic-stricken and desperate. I strongly believe segregation creates a morbid state of mind and drives inmates to kill themselves.

Regrettably, I have lived through two successful inmate suicides. I have changed some of the details and kept others private to ensure the confidentiality of the cases. In the first, the victim's triggering point was his complaint (and very real belief) that another race of segregated inmates was trying to break into his cell and kill him (possibly real, possibly delusional). He denied any thoughts of suicide and in fact stated he was very much trying to stay alive until his release so he could reunite with his family. He had no history of mental illness or suicidality. His only request involved being moved out of segregation and thusly away from his perceived enemies.

In response, we relocated him to our hospital area, with routine staff coverage. A continuous suicide watch did not seem required. The next day, I received a phone call at 2:30 AM from the prison, directing me to go immediately to the institution. When I arrived, I was told of the suicide. I felt terrible. I honestly thought we'd done the right thing for this offender by getting him out of the highly stressful environment he had so genuinely feared. I was instructed to write various memoranda, I was interviewed by several investigators, but at no time did anyone enquire as to my own mental state or express sympathy about my loss. The prison went back to normal operations the following day, but I did not.

The second victim was placed in segregation for speaking harshly to a chaplain regarding his lack of services for a certain religious sect. The inmate was viewed as a leader of the sect and had organized his followers to write letters of complaint to an outside newspaper. The inmate had a history of chaotic relationships, of emotional instability, and of threatening and attempting suicide whenever a girlfriend tried to break off a relationship. He did not exhibit any depression or suicidality while at the prison and was not involved in any outside intimate relationships.

I spoke to him while making rounds in segregation. He was irritable and angry, and he complained about the staff's disrespect for both himself and his religion. He did not engender empathy from me and I viewed him as being rather mean-spirited. Nonetheless, given his history, I recommended he always be double-bunked. About a week later, I was out of state attending the wedding of a friend of my wife when I received another late-night phone call—this time at approximately 3:00 AM. The captain gave me the bad news. The inmate had hung himself.

I was obligated to promptly return to the institution. Upon arrival, I visited the officers in segregation who'd responded to the incident. Not only were they visibly shaken, but they'd also been admonished by an administrator. He'd complained the unit was dirty and insisted it would be "Your jobs…when they (the investigators) get here!"

Over the next couple of days, I, along with some very good staff, were interviewed and interrogated about the incident. During the process, I was made to feel as if I'd entered the cell and hung the inmate myself. At one point, I broke down in tears and the interviewer simply kept questioning me robotically, with no attention to my presence or reaction.

I learned some agonizing lessons in this tragic suicide. First, I'd never before given as much suicide risk weight to anger, irritability, and borderline personality as I did to depression and hopelessness. I now do and I painfully realize the former sometimes may be simply the other side of the same suicide risk coin as the latter. Secondly, I recognize more than ever what a mean-spirited business corrections can be. It often tries to create blame where there is none and shift responsibility from a system or institution to individual employees. At no time during this entire process did anyone ask me how I was doing or offer condolences over the loss. After the interviewers left, the prison returned to normal operations. And once again I did not.

And so this is how I got to suicide behind bars—the relationship work and the research. I am encouraged that so much has been accomplished in terms of knowledge, training, and professional standards over the years. Without Lindsay Hayes, we would still be in the dark ages where suicidal offenders were neglected, mistreated, and abused. I would like to think in some small way my relationship work with offenders has helped make their psychache more bearable and their reasons for living more plentiful.

The hard thing about this work is that you seldom know whom you've truly helped or saved from suicide. Positive feedback is almost non-existent in prison. You're certainly apprised of your failures—even when not under your control—yet no tragedy, trauma, or system re-victimization is more profound than losing an inmate to suicide.

Through much training, writing, speaking, and consulting, I have boldly shared the message that certain characteristics about the incarceration process can lead an inmate to take his or her life. But I'm afraid the message of late simply falls on deaf ears. There has been a disheartening regression in correctional practice over the past several years, to include the expanded use of multi-year segregation for non-violent offenders with added conditions of sensory deprivation such as fogged cell windows.

We live in an era of tough justice, the war on drugs, mandatory minimum sentences, and inmate warehousing. Our country incarcerates more people for longer periods of time than any other nation, yet disproportionately incarcerates people from underprivileged and vulnerable groups such as minorities, the poor, the mentally challenged, and the alcohol and drug addicted. While many political careers are made on the "lock 'em up forever" bandwagon, many, many lives—including offenders, their families, and their children—are broken. For some, the hurt becomes too much to bear and suicide seems like the only way out of a desperately painful, hopeless existence. In spite of the struggle, each one of us must advocate for a justice system that restores reasonable justice for the offender, rational-based sentencing, and hope and real-life opportunities to correct oneself and work toward a better future.

And now for the dry stuff.

2

The Problem of Suicide behind Bars

Suicide represents a serious challenge for the United States correctional system. Lindsay Hayes and the National Center for Institutions and Alternatives (Hayes, 2004, 1995; Hayes & Kajdin, 1981; Hayes & Rowan, 1988) have completed all the major national studies of suicides in jails, prisons, and juvenile detention facilities. As can be seen in Table 2-1, suicide was the leading cause of death

Table 2-1 Some Reported Annual Suicide Rates in Custody, the Mentally Ill, and the General Population

Jails	Prisons	Juvenile Offenders	Adult G.P.	Adolescent G.P.	Mentally Ill
107/100,000(1)	20.6/100,000(2) 13/100,000(7)	10.8/100,000(3) 34/100,000(4)	10.8/100,000(5)	10.8/100,000(3)	167/100,000(6)

1. Hayes, L. M., & Rowan, J. R. (1988). *National study of jail suicides: Seven years later.* Alexandria, VA: NCIA.
2. Hayes, L. M. (1995). *Prison suicide: An overview and guide to prevention.* Mansfield, MA: NCIA.
3. Snyder, H. N. (2005). Is suicide more common inside or outside of juvenile facilities? *Corrections Today* (Feb.2005)
4. Lester, D., & Danto, B. L. (1993). *Suicide behind bars: Prediction and prevention.* Philadelphia, PA: Charles Press.
5. Hoyer, D. L., Smith, B. L., Murphy, S. L., & Kochanet, M. A. (2001). *Deaths: Final data for national vital statistics,* 49. Hyattsville, MD: National Center for Health Statistics.
6. Tanney, B. L. (1992). Mental disorders, psychiatric patients, and suicide. In R. Maris, A. Berman, J. Maltsberger, & R. Yufit (Eds.), *Assessment and prediction of suicide* (pp. 277–320). New York: Guilford
7. Maruschak, L. (2004). HIV in prisons and jails, 2002 U.S. Department of Justice. *Bureau of Justice Statistics Bulletin,* 1-12, 2004 1–12.

in county jails and police lock-ups, and nine times higher than the suicide rate for the general population. The suicide rate for prisoners was reported to be about double that of the general population several years ago, and was the third leading cause of prisoner death (Metzner, Cohen, Grossman, & Wettstein, 1998). The annual prisoner suicide rate appears to have leveled off recently, with an average rate of approximately 13/100,000 inmates for the year 2002 (Maruschak, 2004). The results of a recent study of juvenile offender suicides identified 110 suicides for the period 1995–1999 (Hayes, 2004). Snyder (2005) calculated the annual juvenile offender suicide rate to be about 10.8/100,000, or basically the same as the general adolescent population.

However, Lester and Danto (1993) previously calculated a juvenile offender suicide rate of 34/100,000, or about triple that of the general adolescent population. Interestingly, the suicide rate for juvenile offenders in the Canadian system was noted as 5.5 times higher than the general population of comparable age (Farand, Chagnon, Renaud, & Rivard, 2005). It should be noted that while suicide rates in correctional facilities have been found to be substantially higher than that of the general population, the suicide rates are still substantially less than those of the mentally ill, 167/100,000 (Tanney, 1992).

In addition to suicide, other non-lethal suicidal behaviors are quite prevalent in correctional facilities. Lester and Danto (1993) estimated that for every inmate who kills himself, at least eight inmates would attempt to kill themselves while in custody. Table 2-2 provides prevalence percentages from select studies of suicide ideation and suicide attempts in jail detainees, prisoners, juvenile offenders, psychiatric patients, and the general population.

Table 2-2 Prevalence Percentages of Suicide Ideation and Attempts in Select Jail, Prison, Juveniles Offender, Mentally Ill and General Population Samples.

	Jails	Prisons	Juvenile Detention	General Population	Mentally Ill
Suicide Ideation	77%(1)	35%(2)	9%(3)	8.3%(4)	55%(5)
Suicide Attempts	23%(1)	16%(2)	31%(3)	0.7%(4)	25%(5)

1. Bonner, R. L., & Rich, A. R. (1990). Psychosocial vulnerability, life stress, and suicide ideation in a jail population: A cross-validation study. *Suicide and Life-threatening Behavior*, 20(3), 213–224.
2. Bonner, R. L. (2006a). Stressful segregated housing and psychosocial vulnerability in prison suicide ideators. *Suicide and Life-Threatening Behavior*, In Press.
3. Robertson, A., & Husain, J. (2001). *Prevalence of mental illness and substance abuse disorders among incarcerated juvenile offenders*. Jackson, MS: Mississippi Department of Public Safety and Department of Health.
4. Crosby, A. E., Cheltenham, B. S., & Sacks, J. J. (1999). Incidence of suicidal ideation and behavior in the United States. *Suicide and Life-Threatening Behavior*, 29(2), 131–140.
5. Asnis, G., Friedman, R., & Sanderson, W. (1993). Suicidal behaviors in adult psychiatric outpatients. *American Journal of Psychiatry*, 150, 1009–1015.

In general, the prevalence rates for suicide ideation and attempts are substantially higher in correctional populations than the general population, and at times comparable to that of psychiatric patients. In one study (Bonner, 2006a), 35 percent of prisoners had suicide ideation, which is about four times that of the general population, and 16 percent of prisoners had attempted suicide, which is about six times that of the general population. 77 percent of jail inmates in another study (Bonner & Rich 1990) reported suicide ideation, which is about nine times that of the general population, and 23 percent of jail inmates made a suicide attempt, which is about twenty-three times that of the general population. It should be noted, however, that these studies used small sample sizes, where offenders volunteered to participate. Therefore, the results may not reflect the jail or prison populations as a whole.

In addition to the tragedy that suicidal behavior causes its victims, the impact on others is far reaching. Other inmates who knew the victim are often demoralized and suffer survivor grief and guilt. The traumatic effects on families, parents, siblings, children, and intimates are significant and long standing (Linn-Gust, 2004). The negative impact of suicide on correctional staff is also noteworthy. Good correctional workers, like good police officers (Toch & Grant, 2005), work closely with offenders and develop a caring, problem-solving relationship. Staff members are also traumatized by inmate suicidal behavior, and as is the case with many of the "helping professions," often suffer survivor grief and guilt. Unfortunately, the finger pointing nature of the correctional business (Bonner, 2005a) and litigious nature of our society (Robertson, 2004) too often create further stress and worry for staff suicide survivors, further deepening their trauma and emotional suffering.

3

Risk Factors of the Suicide Process

During the past thirty years, much information about suicidal behavior behind bars has been accumulated through observation, empirical research, and theoretical development. We are now able to point to various "risk factors" associated with suicide completions, attempts, and ideation. These risk factors may be categorized into three types: *Distal risk factors, proximate risk factors*, and *immediate risk factors*.

Distal risk factors refer to those victim characteristics that are distant or removed from the recent or current dynamics leading up to the suicidal behavior. Jail suicide victims, for example, tend to be male, white, unemployed, socially isolated, younger, non-violent offenders, substance abusers, and not mentally ill (Gunn, Robertson, Dell, & Way, 1978; Hayes & Rowan, 1988). Prison suicide victims, on the other hand, tend to be older, white, male, violent, socially isolated, with histories of mental illness and suicide attempts, and serving twenty years to life in maximum security facilities (Bonner, 2006b; Hayes, 1995; Lester & Danto, 1993; White & Schimmel, 1995). Juvenile victims, however, tend to have histories of mental illness, suicide attempts, and emotional/physical/sexual abuse (Hayes, 2004a).

In terms of proximate suicide risk factors, or those factors in close time and situation to the suicide action, the majority of prison, jail, and juvenile detention victims were housed in isolation/segregation at the time of their act and used bed clothing to hang themselves (Hayes, 2004, 1995; Hayes & Rowan, 1988). For jail victims, most of the victims were intoxicated and had completed suicide within the first twenty-four hours of incarceration. For prisons, victims tended to have problems with other inmates, suffer from active depression or mental illness, and had chronic and acute stress (He, Felthous, Holzer, Nathan, & Veasey, 2001; Salive, Smith, & Brewer, 1989; White & Schimmel, 1995). The majority of these victims were suffering from depression at the time of their deaths (Hayes, 1995).

In terms of immediate suicide risk factors, the domain of the suicidal mental state is the focus, as this will ultimately plunge a person into suicidal action. Common risk factors identified from the general clinical suicidology literature suggest the suicide idea and its progression from intention to contemplation combines with decision-making, the death wish, psychache, and hopelessness to be the key components of the suicide mind state (Bonner, 2005b, 2001). Toch (1992), in studying the effects of the isolation associated with segregation housing, described the "isolation panic" that plunges an inmate into despair and suicide as follows: "The reaction to isolation is a panic state. It is a feeling of abandonment, a back to the wall, an intolerable emptiness, helplessness, and tension. It is a physical reaction for release, or as a need to escape at all costs." (p.52)

As the state of the suicidal mind is at the core of immediate suicide risk, several studies have been conducted to look at mind state correlations of suicide intention in offenders (See Table 3-1).

Table 3-1 Correlates of the Inmate Suicidal Mind State from Selected Studies

	Confinement Stress	Reasons for Living	Depression	Hopelessnes:	Attempt History	Psy. Tment Hs
Suicide Intention Jails (1, 2)	.41*	-.54*	.61*	76*	N/A	N/A
Suicide Intention Prisons (3)	.21*	-.43*	.54*	.61*	.62*	.41*

*p<.05

1. Bonner, R. L., & Rich, A. R. (1990). Psychosocial vulnerability, life stress, and suicide ideation in a jail population: A cross-validation study. *Suicide and Life-Threatening Behavior*, 20(3), 213–224.
2. Bonner, R. L., & Rich, A. R. (1992). Cognitive vulnerability and hopelessness among correctional inmates. *Journal of Offender Rehabilitation*, 17(3/4), 113–122
3. Bonner, R. L. (2006a). Stressful segregation housing and psychosocial vulnerability in prison suicide ideators. *Suicide and Life-Threatening Behavior*, In Press.

In general, inmates at risk for suicide intention share several characteristics. These include life stress, depression, hopelessness regarding the future, a history of suicide attempts, treatment for depression or mental illness, few reasons for living, and ascription to a number of pro-suicide beliefs. In terms of isolation, a recent study found prison inmates housed in segregation had significantly higher levels of depression and suicide intention than inmates housed in general population, independent of mental health treatment or suicide attempt history (Bonner, 2006a).

Table 3-2 outlines the common risk factors for the suicide process behind bars and should serve as a guide for risk screening and assessment.

Table 3-2 Some Common Risk Factors of Suicide Behind Bars

Immediate Mental State Risk Factors:
- Suicidal Ideation, Contemplation, and Planning
- Acquiring a method
- Wishes and fantasies about death
- Psychache (intolerable emotional pain)
- Isolation panic (segregation induced)
- Hopelessness

Proximate Risk Factors:
- Segregation
- Intoxication
- Psychosis (with suicide command hallucinations or delusions)
- Depression, mania, rage, anxiety, mental illness
- Pro-suicide beliefs, suicide fantasies
- Limited adaptive beliefs, reasons for living
- Stage of suicide process (ideation, contemplation, planning/decision-making, giving away possessions, writing a good-bye letter)
- -Acute stress (loss, victimization, etc.)

Distal Risk Factors:
- Chronic stress
- History of substance abuse
- History of mental illness
- History of suicide attempts
- History of physical, emotional, or sexual abuse
- Family history of mental illness and/or suicide
- First time jail offenders/non-violent offense/drug & alcohol related
- First twenty-four hours of jail confinement
- Violent, maximum-security prisoners doing twenty years to life sentences
- Older age, male, white prisoners
- Younger age, male, white jail detainees
- Socially isolated
- Lack of cultural and/or religious anti-suicide values

Given the multitude of risk factors for suicide in general, and behind bars in particular, an integrative, organized framework is needed to account for the relationship among risk factors. In addition, this framework needs to explain the process by which a given inmate under certain life and incarceration circumstances contemplates, plans, and decides to end his or her life at a certain point in confinement. In this pursuit, a stress-diathesis process/state of mind model of suicide risk has been developed (Bonner, 2006a, 2005b, 2001; Bonner & Rich, 1992, 1990). Suicide is defined as a developmental, coping process of stages, to include Stage 1: Passive Suicide Ideation, Stage 2: Suicide Contemplation (detailed cost/benefit thinking), Stage 3: Suicide Planning and Decision-Making, and Stage 4: Suicide Action.

As an inmate progresses through these stages, his or her suicide risk increases as the result of a hopeless state of mind (Beck, Weissman, Lester, & Trexler, 1974; Beck, Steer, Beck, & Newman, 1993). The suicidal mind state is thought to vary in intention and intensity, depending upon the variable influence of a number of biopsychosocial vulnerabilities (or risk factors) in transaction with environmental demands, life stress, and the perceived degree of hopelessness. Over time, this process of coping interactions—accompanied by repeated failures and emotional upset—is thought to result in psychache and intolerable emotional pain (Orbach, Mikulciner, Gilboa-Schectman & Siroto, 1993; Shneidman, 2004, 2001), which then plunges the inmate into suicide action as a desperate attempt to escape unbearable, psychological pain.

Applying this model to a volunteer sample of jail inmates (Bonner & Rich, 1992, 1990), the combination of social isolation, pro-suicide beliefs, few or no reasons for living, and jail incarceration stress accounted for 51 percent of the variance in inmate suicide intention. In addition, significant interactions between isolation, irrational (pro-suicide) beliefs, and jail stress were also found, independent of depressed mood.

In extending this research to a volunteer sample of prisoners (Bonner, 2006a), select psychosocial vulnerability factors—namely mental health problem treatment history, suicide attempt lethality history, reasons for living, depression, and hopelessness—were studied in interaction with stressful conditions of segregated housing. The combination of suicide attempt lethality history and hopelessness best accounted for suicide intention in inmates. In addition, significant interactions between the vulnerability factors and appraised segregation stress were found. In other words, it was those inmates who were hopeless, with a suicide attempt history and a mental health treatment history, and who appraised segregation as stressful who were most at risk for suicide intention, independent of depressed mood.

4

Suicide Risk Screening and Assessment

In reviewing the process model of inmate suicide risk, several important implications for screening and assessment are noteworthy: (1) Assessment is a short-term endeavor of risk estimation, not prediction, based on a snapshot of the particular constellation of biopsychosocial vulnerabilities (or risk factors) of a specific inmate, in a particular situation, and at a given point of time. (2) Screening and assessment are ongoing and dynamic, as is the process of suicide. (3) The core of assessment is the suicidal mind state, which includes the suicide stages (ideation, contemplation, planning and decision-making), the level and threshold of psych-ache, the wish and fantasy to die, isolation panic (segregation-induced), and hopelessness. (4) The secondary level of risk assessment deals with the proximate risk factors, or the specific stress-coping vulnerabilities and failures that lead to psychache and the suicidal mind. Key factors in this domain are pro-suicide ideas, suicide fantasies, active mental illness, psychotic-suicide themes, depression, rage, mania, intoxication, acute stress or problems, and segregated housing. (5) The distal risk factors should then be assessed, to include histories of mental health problems, suicide attempts, substance abuse, chronic stress, first time jail offenders, violent maximum-security prisoners, physically/emotionally/sexually abused juvenile offenders, family history of suicide or mental illness, religious or cultural backgrounds which do not hold anti-suicide values, and other taxing demographics such as sex, age, and race. (6) Throughout these steps of assessment, the presence and availability of protectors or buffers, such as social support, psychosocial resources, coping strengths and adaptive beliefs, should be identified and considered as minimizers of suicide risk.

Screening for inmate suicide risk essentially answers the question, is this inmate at risk for suicide? All correctional staff can and should be expected to screen inmates for suicide risk during admission and at different high-risk periods (e.g., relationship loss, losing an appeal, conviction/sentencing, victimization) and in high-risk places (e.g., segregation). The answer to the screening question is affirmative when an inmate presents any of the immediate mental state, proximate, or distal risk factors. In general, immediate mental state and proximate risk factors should result in an immediate referral for a formal suicide risk assessment by a mental health professional.

In the event the inmate cannot be evaluated immediately, suicide precautions should be implemented. For the presence of immediate mental state suicide risk factors (e.g., suicide planning and decision-making, giving away possessions, communicating intent to die or saying good-bye, severe emotional pain (poor sleep, poor appetite, psychomotor agitation, mood swings, depression, rages, isolation/panic/segregation), poor emotional controls via psychosis, intoxication, impulsivity, and hopelessness, this inmate should be placed under a constant (continuous) staff watch until he or she can be formally evaluated by a mental health clinician.

For the presence of proximate risk factors (e.g., depression, acute stress, mental illness, ineffective coping or problem-solving, suicide thinking (without plan or decision), this inmate should be housed with other inmates, double-bunked if in cell or segregation (segregation should be avoided at all costs unless there is a danger to others) and closely monitored by staff at specified intervals such as every fifteen minutes until he or she can be formally evaluated for suicide risk by a mental health clinician. For the inmate that simply presents distal risk factors, a routine referral to mental health services is indicated with no special precautions other than non-isolated housing.

While suicide risk screening uses the presence of risk factors to determine an inmate's risk for suicide, suicide risk assessment attempts to determine the level of suicide risk in the immediate future. The Stage-Modality System (SMS) of suicide risk assessment is offered as a working guide to help the clinician in this process. Figure 4-1 outlines a model to represent this system by suicide stages and biopsychosocial vulnerability modalities.

Figure 4-1 Stage-Modality System of Inmate Suicide Risk Assessment: A Working Guide

Extreme Hopelessness and Psychache Threshold Pressed >IMMINENT RISK>Stage 4-Suicide Action

Stage 3 Suicide Planning and Decision-Making and Affective State > HIGH RISK

- Suicide plans, acquiring a method, preparing (making a will, saying goodbye, giving away possessions)
- Psychache threshold
- Depression, mania, rage, agitation, isolation panic (segregation-induced)
- Influenced/intoxicated with mood-altering substances
- Mood dysregulation/weak controls
- Acute stress/crisis state

Stage 2: Suicide Contemplation and Mental State > MODERATE RISK

- Suicidal thinking, cost/benefit analysis
- Wish to die
- Pro-suicide beliefs
- Few adaptive beliefs, reasons for living
- Suicide fantasies
- Psychotic suicide themes
- Helpless/hopeless images

Stage 1: Passive Suicide Ideation and Psychosocialbiological History Context >LOW RISK

- Brief, fleeting thoughts of suicide
- Maladaptive coping history
  - Personal/familial history of depression, mental illness, and suicidality
- Childhood physical, emotional, and/or sexual abuse
- Chronic stress
- Isolated, lack of social support
- Lack of cultural/religious anti-suicide values
- Other taxing sociodemographic factors

Note: The foregoing is adapted in part from *A psychotherapist's dark journey into the suicidal mind: A relationship approach to understanding and healing* (p. 44) by R. L. Bonner (2005b). Copyright by the iUniverse Press. Used with permission.
**The reader should understand this system is simply a working guide to help clinicians in the process of suicide risk assessment. Clinicians should access as many data sources for each individual case as possible. Regular professional training and consultation are critically important for clinicians involved in the suicide risk assessment of offenders.

Again, the suicide stages are passive ideation, suicide contemplation, suicide planning and decision-making, and suicide action. Risk level can in part be estimated based on where an inmate is in this stage process: Stage 1: Low Risk, Stage 2: Moderate Risk, Stage 3: High Risk, and Stage 4: Imminent Risk (with a plan, method available, psychache threshold met with break-down in controls such as psychotic processing, intoxication, inability to regulate/control emotion).

The M.A.P. guide was devised to help the clinician target the key modalities of the suicide process, namely Mental State, Affective State, and Psychosocialbiological History Context (Bonner, 1992b, 1990). The mental state domain refers to the thoughts and perceptions associated with suicide intention, including the wish to die (vs. the wish to live), suicide contemplation and planning, suicide fantasies, pro-suicide beliefs, reasons for living, active psychosis with suicidal themes, and expectations of hopelessness. The affective state modality refers to the nature, level, and threshold for emotional pain or psychache for including depression, mania, rage, agitation, isolation panic, and intoxication or influence by mood altering drugs or alcohol. The psychosocialbiological history context principally refers to the person's coping history, including personal or familial history of depression, mental illness, or suicide attempts. There appears to be a unique biological/genetic pattern to the suicide process, involving in part the neurotransmitter serotonin (Roy, 2001). People tend to recycle through the suicide process repeatedly, thereby increasing coping failures and upsetting and pressing the psychache threshold, which eventually will result in suicide for some. As with inmates, people in general having a history of suicide ideation, contemplation, planning, and attempting are at much higher risk for eventual suicide (Linehan, 1999).

Suicide risk assessment usually begins with a clinical interview. The reliability and validity of the information obtained from the inmate will be in direct proportion to the quality of the relationship between the clinician and the inmate (Bonner, 2005b). The clinician must show genuine concern and compassion for the inmate's emotional pain and provide a validating experience for the inmate. When this transpires, the inmate will most often be very open and forthcoming about his or her life story and the suicide process, namely because he or she is generally ambivalent about wanting to die but wants help and relief for his or her problem and suffering. To assist in the interview, a number of suicide risk instruments have been developed to more systematically capture the inmate's mental and affective state (See Table 4-1). In addition to the interview, the clinician should access as

Table 4-1 Some Common Suicide Risk Instruments

CORRECTIONAL POPULATIONS
Suicide Risk Assessment, Intake Screening Form, Arresting/Transporting Officer Questionnaire
Hayes, L. M. and the National Center for Institutions and Alternatives (2005). *Jail Suicide/Mental Health Update*, 13(4), 13, 13–18.
Suicide Risk Indicators Checklist for RMU/SMU
Couturier, L., & Maue, F. R. (2000). Suicide prevention initiatives in a large statewide department of corrections: A full-court press to save lives. *Jail Suicide/Mental Health Update*, 9(4), 1–8.
The New York State Suicide Prevention Screening Guidelines
Sherman, L. G., & Morschauser, P. C. (1989). Screening for suicide risk in inmates. *Psychiatric Quarterly*, 60, 119–138.

MENTAL STATE OF SUICIDE INTENTION
Scale for Suicide Ideators
Beck, A. T., Kovacs, M., & Weissman, A. (1979). Assessment of suicidal ideation: The Scale for Suicide Ideators. *Journal of Consulting and Clinical Psychology*, 47, 343–352.
Suicide Intent Scales
Beck, A. T., Schuyler, D., & Herman, I. (1974). Development of suicide intent scales. In A. T. Beck, H. L. P. Resnick, & D. J. Lettieri (Eds.), *The prediction of suicide* (pp. 45–56). Bowie, MD: Charles Press.
Suicidal Ideation Questionnaires
Reynolds, W. M. (1987). *Suicidal Ideation Questionnaires*. Odessa, FL: Psychological Assessment Resources.
Beck Hopelessness Scale
Beck, A. T. (1987). *Beck Hopelessness Scale*. San Antonio: TX: The Psychological Corporation.
Reasons for Living Inventory
Linehan, M. (1985). Reasons for living inventory. In P. A. Keller & L. G. Ritt (Eds.), *Innovations in clinical practice* (Vol. 4, pp 321–330). Sarasota, FL: Professional Resource Exchange
AFFECTIVE STATE OF SUICIDE INTENTION
The Psychological Pain Assessment Scale
Shneidman, E. (1999). The psychological pain assessment scale. *Suicide and Life-Threatening Behavior*, 29, 287–294.
The Revised Beck Depression Inventory
Beck, A. T., & Steer, R. A. (1987). *Manual for the revised Beck Depression Inventory*. San Antonia, TX: The Psychological Corporation.

many data sources as are available, including previous mental health records and interviews with family members, significant others, inmate peers, the arresting officer, or any other staff members who know and have worked with this inmate. It has been this author's experience that the gut reaction and feelings of the correctional officer most familiar with a given inmate are often more valuable than any other data source, as his or her contacts and observations are continuous and highly representative of the inmate's mental and affective states.

5

Process Interventions for the Suicidal Inmate

The process model of inmate suicide, as outlined in Chapter 3, suggests that interventions need to be tailored to the stage of the suicidal inmate as well as the unique multimodal systems of the person. Lazarus (1995, 1989) has noted the importance of "sequential firing" in the person's coping transactions, and for our purposes the inmate's transactions across Mental State, Affective State, and Psychosocial Context systems or M.A.P. (Bonner, 1992b, 2001, 1990; Bonner & Michalik-Bonner, 1996). Some modalities will be more salient for certain inmates, but not others. Moreover, intervention into one modality often activates change in other modalities. Figure 5-1 outlines possible modality interventions for the suicidal inmate at specific stages of the suicide process. Each case is unique, and assessment and intervention will need to be individualized and dynamic. Clinicians are strongly encouraged to regularly participate in professional training in the assessment and treatment of suicidality and to always seek consultation when unsure or progress seems limited.

Figure 5-1 Some Stage Specific Process Interventions for the Suicidal Inmate

Stage 4 Suicide Act-M.A.P. Interventions -Emergency Medical Care
-Constant Suicide Watch
-Comprehensive M.A.P. Assessment
-Consider Psychiatric Hospitalization
-Intensify Mental Health and Psychiatric Tx
-If no improvement, consider ECT

Stage 3 Suicide Planning and Decision Making-Affective Interventions

PsychacheThreshold -Target depression, agitation, and psychache with cognitive and pharmacological interventions
-Improve mood modulation and affect tolerance via mood stabilizing medications, SSRI's and

Hopelessness -Dialectical Behavior Therapy -If psychache threshold met or weak controls, place on constant
suicide watch. If not and engaged in pro-living treatment contract, keep in general population

Stage 2 Suicide Contemplation and Mental State Interventions
-Examine the suicide idea, costs/benefits, intentions, and wishes to live/die.
-Challenge and disrupt suicide assumptions, irrational beliefs, tunnel vision, cognitive distortions, and
fantasies of the suicide idea
-Teach problem-solving skills
-Access/build reasons for living and psychosocial supports
-Provide bibliotherapy
-House in general population with other inmates and routine monitoring

Stage 1 Passive Suicide Ideation-Psychosocial Context Interventions
-Increase family, peer, and staff supports
-Participate in self-improvement and purpose-driven programming (faith-based)
-Resolve problem trigger
-House in general population with other inmates and routine monitoring

Note: The foregoing is adapted in part from *A psychotherapist's dark journey into the suicidal mind: A relationship approach to understanding and healing* (p. 44) by R. L. Bonner (2005b). Copyright by iUniverse Press. Used by permission.
**The reader should realize the above figure is simply a working guide to process interventions with a suicidal inmate. Each case is unique and the treatment plan will need to be individualized and dynamic based on the mental, affective, and psychosocial processes of a given inmate. Clinicians are strongly encouraged to attend regular professional training on the treatment of suicidality as well as seek consultation when unsure or progress seems limited.

Stage 1 and Passive Suicide Ideation

Psychosocial Context Interventions

For inmates at the stage of passive suicide ideation (a common experience by jail and prison inmates according to Bonner, 2006a; Bonner & Rich, 1992, 1990), psychosocial interventions such as peer feedback and support, family contacts and support, and inmate stress management-building programs and problem-solving skills are helpful. In addition, accessing or building cultural and religious beliefs that have anti-suicide values will help the passive suicide ideator move on to adaptive, life-oriented problem solving. Protective factors of social supports and reasons for living buffer the inmate suicide ideator from stress and problems, and often offer guidance toward successful problem resolution.

Staff Monitoring and Housing

Special staff monitoring is not usually required at this stage, other than the standard thirty-minute checks for all inmates (Danto, 1997). Inmates at this stage should be housed within general population with other inmates, and not housed in isolation. No formal mental health intervention will be needed unless there is an underlying mental or mood disorder. These inmates generally will not need professional follow-up unless there is a history of the suicide process, or they come from suicide at-risk groups, such as suicide attempters, the mentally ill, or families with histories of mental illness or suicide. In these cases, periodic follow-ups by mental health staff should be provided to determine if the inmate has advanced the suicide process to another stage. Having a "hot list" of such inmates with a history of such factors can be helpful to alert other staff to those who need closer attention or monitoring, especially if being placed in segregation (Bonner, 1998).

Stage 2 and Active Suicide Contemplation

Mental State Interventions

At Stage 2, the inmate is starting to seriously think about suicide, going through a cost-benefit analysis of living and dying, and anticipating the likelihood or unlikelihood of successful problem resolution. The mental state is the primary area of intervention at this stage, wherein counseling and bibliotherapy can systematically target such mental factors as suicide intention, wishes to live and die, tunnel vision, ineffective problem-solving skills, reasons for living, helpless and hopeless images, and suicide fantasies. The basic goal at this stage is to challenge and dispute pro-suicide thoughts and replace them with adaptive, rational beliefs, logical decision-making, and ultimately successful problem solving with the effect of a reduction in hopeless expectancies.

Bibliotherapy

In terms of bibliotherapy, Paul Quinnett's (1997) *Suicide: The Forever Decision* speaks directly to the suicidal person in Stage 2 of suicide contemplation. He captures the eye and mind of the suicide contemplator and understands why suicide has come to make sense for the suicidal person. Dr. Quinnett then challenges the contemplator to think through the consequences if he or she was to commit suicide, such as the impact on family, friends, and children. He also takes a rational, evidence based approach in helping the reader determine if suicide actually would solve his or her problem, and if the suicide fantasy is likely to be fulfilled with the contemplator's suicide. Finally, he offers alternative thinking and experimentation with new behaviors to assess the impact on the problem and the suicide idea. The reader leaves feeling convinced that Dr. Quinnett deeply understands the reasons for contemplating suicide, but genuinely believes rational thinking, problem-solving skills, and accessing psychosocial support will most often result in the contemplator deciding his or her reasons for living far outweigh the reasons for dying.

Another very helpful book for the suicide contemplator is *Choosing to Live: How to Defeat Suicide Through Cognitive Therapy*, written by Thomas Ellis and Cory Newman (1996). In a sense, this book takes Quinnett's work to the next level by actually teaching a step by step therapy program for the person in the suicide process. The reader is taught specific therapeutic strategies in modifying cognitive distortions, irrational beliefs, pro-suicide beliefs, and suicide fantasies. In addition, the work provides a number of behavioral exercises and self-monitoring instruments to facilitate systematic, skill-building, life-oriented coping.

These books can be given by a variety of correctional staff members (e.g., officers, correctional counselors, nurses, supervisors, pastors, and mental health providers) to an inmate who appears in distress, facing a crisis, and/or thinking about suicide. The format of the books could easily be integrated into a correctional counseling group for new inmates adjusting to incarceration.

Distributing this material to high inmate traffic areas such as housing units, chapels, and educational facilities would serve as a proactive step to suicide prevention. Also, issuing such books to inmates who come from high risk populations such as first timers, jail lock-up inmates, previous suicide attempters, the mentally ill, and all inmates housed in segregation could become standard practice.

Cognitive Therapy

As discussed previously, a variety of correctional staff members can make available the resources needed to assist inmates contemplating suicide. If such resources are unavailable or the inmate does not exit the suicide process, the role of the mental health provider becomes more important in analyzing the inmate's cost/benefit analysis and implementing specific cognitive strategies to outweigh death over life decisions. In this process, Figure 5-2 provides a Self-Monitoring Suicide Contemplation Analysis for the inmate who is contemplating suicide.

Figure 5-2 Suicide Contemplation M.A.P. Monitoring Schedule

Date	Psychosocial Context/Situation	Mental State Thoughts	Affective State/Emotions	Alternative Thoughts

The inmate records the date of the contemplation, the situation (or psychosocial context), the thoughts he or she is having in terms of suicide and the costs and benefits perceived, the associated emotions, and finally brainstorming solutions to the trigger problem and what other alternatives will outweigh the cost/benefit analysis to life-oriented coping and eventually lead to an exit from the suicide process. Table 5-1 outlines ten common underlying pro-suicide beliefs associated with the contemplation of suicide and the rational evidence that counters these beliefs.

Table 5-1 Some Common Inmate Pro-Suicide Beliefs of the Suicide Process and Refutation

Pro-Suicide Beliefs & Refutation

Others will be better off if I am dead. Where is the evidence? Most people suffer trauma when someone they know or love commits suicide. Don't they at least deserve input into your decision since it is you who says they will be better?

I am too much of a burden to my family. How do you know that? Have they told you the burden would be less if you were dead? Most of the time the burden of suicide is much worse on children and family members. Have you at least involved them in your decision?

Everyone has screwed me over, now it's my turn to show them. Has absolutely everyone in your life done you wrong? Can't you think of anybody who has done you good or treated you well? Do you really believe your suicide will show your enemies? I don't think your enemies would even be fazed by your death, or they might just think you're crazy.

I can't do anymore time in jail. How did you arrive at that decision? Look at how much time you've already done. What about all these guys who are doing life and don't have the chances you will. What about your children? You can't do any more time for them? What will happen to them when you kill yourself?

My family is gonna get a lot of money from this place when I go. Maybe, but did you know most prison suicide lawsuits are ruled in favor of the prison? Even if your family was awarded money, how are they going to feel when you're dead? and they think you did it because of them.

My future sucks, I got nothing to live for. While your present life might suck, how do you know your future will? Usually, the bad times will eventually get better. You have nothing to live for? What about your family, children, and your friends here? What faith are you? What does it teach about suicide? What about *our* relationship? It would matter a great deal to me if you killed yourself. I care about you.

The prison made me this way and now I'll give them what they want. Can you tell me how the prison made you this way? What about the good parts? Your concern for your peers, your children, your family? Do you mean to tell me you have no control or influence into who you are? How is it that the prison wants you to kill yourself? If what you're saying is true, would it really care or matter? So you're going to let a system like this make you take your life? It seems like you want them to win.

At least I'll be out of here when I die. Actually, you won't be anywhere. You won't exist. Do you have any beliefs about a life hereafter? If so, where will you go? What if you go to another prison—an eternal prison? There are no guarantees, you know.

I'm not gonna have someone do me in when I can do it myself. What are the chances someone is going to do you in? If you have a problem, you know I can try to get you transferred. What will your enemy think if you kill yourself? What about your family? Is this person (enemy) really worth you taking your life and hurting your family?

It's only going to get worse and I can't take it anymore. How do you know it's going to get worse? Couldn't it get better? What do you mean you can't take it? Look what you've gone through so far, and for your kids and family. People have a powerful survival instinct and have coped with situations a lot worse than yours. You really *can* take it. What you're saying is that you don't *want* to take it, regardless what it does to those who love and care about you.

Note: The foregoing is partially adapted from *A psychotherapist's dark journey into the suicidal mind: A relationship approach to understanding and healing* (p.37) by R. L. Bonner (2005b). Copyright by the iUniverse Press. Used with permission.

Clinicians will need to focus on the presence of the pro-suicide beliefs and use therapy dialogue and homework "experimentation" to challenge and disrupt the suicide contemplation of the inmate. Correctional mental health care providers are referred to a state of the art treatment manual for the suicide process entitled *Treating Suicidal Behavior: An Effective, Time Limited Approach* written by David Rudd, Thomas Joiner, and Hajan Rajab (2001). This work outlines stage-specific cognitive treatment strategies, in a session-by-session format, to systematically modify the mental state of suicide.

Other Treatments

In terms of the suicidal mind's state of contemplation, mental health clinicians will also need to rule out the presence of an underlying thought disorder such as psychosis. For some mentally ill inmates, suicide may have its meaning in a fixed delusional system, such as the inmate who believes "I must die to defeat Satan and the evil spirits." In such a case, the primary focus of treatment is obviously to reduce the psychotic symptoms, most often with the use of antipsychotic medication. This then facilitates the inmate exiting the suicide process (Salzman, 1999).

Secondary interventions at the stage of suicide contemplation, as outlined in Stage 1, would involve accessing and building social/family supports and participating in self-help and faith-based programming. Such supports buffer an inmate from the effects of stress and problems in living. Also, a buddy system may be used with the suicide contemplator's consent by pairing a trained inmate peer with the inmate suicide contemplator to provide support and corrective dialogue regarding problem-solving, doing time, and purpose-driven living (Bonner, 1992a, 1992b; Lester & Danto, 1993).

Staff Monitoring and Housing

As long as the inmate at Stage 2 is engaged in an intervention process (e.g., buddy system, bibliotherapy, cognitive therapy, correctional group counseling, or other psychological programming) and housed with other inmates in the general population—as opposed to being segregated—only routine staff monitoring is indicated. However, if the inmate is currently in segregation or unable or unwilling to participate in intervention, closer staff monitoring at fifteen-minute intervals and double bunking are recommended.

Stage 3 and Suicide Planning and Decision-Making Affective State Interventions

Mental Health Treatment

For inmates at Stage 3 who have made the decision to attempt suicide and developed a plan to do so, prompt, structured treatment is indicated. At this stage, the most compelling modality for professional intervention is the affective state, namely depression, mania, anger, rage, panic, despair, and hopelessness—the inmate's emotional pain. Shneidman (2001) has summarized the affective state of the suicidal person as "psychache," intolerable emotional pain that must be relieved to reverse the suicide process and prevent a suicide attempt or completion. Intensive cognitive-behavioral therapy and the use of antidepressant and/or anti-anxiety medications are effective in providing affective relief, although such action may take time to produce symptom relief, and, therefore, requires close monitoring of the suicidal inmate (Barlow, 2004; Medina, 1998; Salzman, 1999).

In addition, such medications should be tightly controlled through pill-line procedures to prevent the inmate from "cheeking" (concealing medications in the cheek or under their tongue) his or her medication to prevent an accidental or intentional overdose. Tricylic antidepressants and benzodiazepines should rarely be provided to the suicidal inmate, given the potential for fatal overdose (Salzman, 1999).

At Stage 3, the mental health clinician must regularly assess the lethality of the planned method, intention to die, and opportunities for rescue during the planned method, and the inmate's history of suicide action (past intention and lethality of attempt). If these factors are present, the inmate's ability and desire to regulate and tolerate emotional pain must be thoroughly examined. If the inmate's controls are intact and the psychache threshold has not been reached, and he or she is willing to receive therapy in a life-sustaining relationship, then he or she can be housed in general population (with careful staff monitoring at fifteen-minute intervals).

Within the context of a well-established, therapeutic relationship, a "Pro-Living Relationship Contract" can be used in dialogue and writing to help the inmate work on living and reversing the suicide process (See Figure 5-3). If the inmate is intoxicated, psychotic, poorly controlled, and/or unable to engage in a treatment contract, he or she should be placed on a

Figure 5-3 Pro-Living Relationship Agreement

Because of our work together, I, _____, realize that you care about me and don't want to see anything happen that would harm me. Because I care about you and our relationship, I promise that I will not act on my suicide decision and I will plan and do my best to focus on living, and not dying. You have my word that if I start to feel worse or if I think I am going to lose control, I will immediately go to a staff member to have them contact you. I also realize from our work together that I care about_____ _____, and would not want to hurt or traumatize them by acting on my suicide plan.

Agreed upon by:

_____
Patient Date

_____
Therapist Date

**Note: Clinicians should not simply accept this agreement as assurance that an inmate will not act on his or her suicide intention. It is the clinician's ongoing assessment of suicide risk and the quality of his or her relationship with a suicidal inmate that will dictate the course of intervention and the need for suicide precautions.
Note: The foregoing is adapted in part from *A psychotherapist's dark journey into the suicidal mind: A relationship approach to understanding and healing* (p. 32) by R. L. Bonner (2005b). Copyright by the iUniverse Press. Used with permission.

suicide watch under constant staff observation. The cell should be devoid of fixtures that could be used to inflict injury, and it should be comfortably designed with bright colors and floor and wall carpeting. An observation window or door that allows close observation and quality interaction between the suicidal inmate and the staff watcher should be provided. He or she should remain on watch until the inmate's mood is improved and regulated and he or she is willing to engage in a pro-living relationship agreement. Figure 5-4 provides a "Self-Analysis of Mood Controls" to help the inmate suicide planner and the therapist determine his or her level of control and ability to tolerate emotional pain.

Figure 5-4 Self-Analysis of Mood Controls

What are the reasons you have not acted on your suicide decision and plan?

....

....

....

What would it take for you to act on your decision and plan?

....

....

How likely is that? ....

How likely is it that you will attempt suicide today? ....

     Tomorrow? ....

     In a few days? ....

     In a week? ....

     In two weeks? ....

     In a month? ....

In terms of your depression and emotional pain, will you be able to tolerate it today? ....

     Tomorrow? ....

     In a few days? ....

     In a week? ....

     In two weeks? ....

     In a month? ....

How much more can you take before you will lose control? ....

Note: The foregoing is adapted from *A psychotherapist's dark journey into the suicidal mind: A relationship approach to understanding and healing* (p.30) by R. L. Bonner (2005b). Copyright by the iUniverse Press. Used with permission.

For mood regulation, the selective serotonin reuptake inhibitor (SSRI) antidepressants are thought to have the added benefit of stabilizing low serotonin levels associated with mood swings. They also impact tolerance, dysregulation, and the aggression linked with suicide (Van Pragg, 1991). Also, mood-stabilizing medications are useful in reducing mood swings and mood cycling, and improving frustration tolerance (Roy, 1991).

Also for mood regulation, Marsha Linehan (1987) has developed "Dialectical Behavior Therapy." According to Dr. Linehan, the key components of this treatment are: "Acknowledgment of the patient's sense of emotional desperation (validation strategies); a matter of fact attitude about current and previous parasuicidal and other dysfunctional behaviors…an active attempt to 'reframe' suicidal and other dysfunctional behaviors as part of the patient's learned problem-solving repertoire, and continuing effort to focusing therapy on active problem-solving." Additionally, Dr. Linehan states, "The therapist actively teaches emotional regulation, interpersonal effectiveness, distress tolerance, and self-management skills…" (p. 272).

Edwin Shneidman's recent *Autopsy of a Suicidal Mind* (2004) poignantly captures the therapeutic essence of doing whatever it takes to make unbearable emotional pain at least barely bearable and somehow tolerable.

Staff Monitoring and Housing

If the inmate suicide planner is engaged in treatment and his or her controls are intact, housing with other inmates in the general population is recommended. At this level, staff should still more closely observe this inmate, such as at fifteen-minute intervals, until he or she has retreated from the suicide decision and plan. If the inmate is not engaged in treatment, mood is unregulated, and/or he or she is intoxicated, the inmate should be placed on suicide watch in a safe, therapeutic cell with constant staff observation and interaction. In terms of bed materials and clothing, suicide-proof blankets and smocks can be used which can be purchased through several companies.

Stage 4: Suicide Action

Intensive M.A.P. Interventions

For the inmate who has reached Level 4 of suicide action, emergency medical care is clearly the first step of intervention. All correctional staff should be trained in responding to medical emergencies and performing CPR if indicated until medical staff arrives. For bleeding, pressure with a barrier should be applied to the wound until medical staff arrives. For hanging, the inmate should be immediately cut down and placed lying on the floor with his or her head protected. All institutions should have specifically designed "911 Rescue Tools," including hook-shaped knives that can quickly cut through most fibrous materials, but cannot be used as a weapon because the blade resides within the frame (Hayes, 1991). Standard CPR procedures should then be implemented if the inmate is not breathing or does not have a pulse. Once medically stabilized, a comprehensive mental health treatment plan needs to be developed that targets all M.A.P. modalities (i.e., Mental State, Affective State, Psychosocial Context). Interventions for early stages may also need to be reapplied.

Some critical issues need to be considered in treatment planning. First, can the inmate still be successfully treated on an outpatient basis in the jail or prison setting? Is he or she willing to engage in treatment and agree to a pro-living treatment plan? Is he or she relieved to be alive and does he or she regret the suicide action? If not, does he or she need the treatment and monitoring intensity of psychiatric hospitalization? If the inmate is unwilling to consent to treatment, efforts should be made to petition a court for involuntary hospitalization and treatment. In the event the inmate suffers from mental illness and has been in treatment, the effectiveness of the treatment plan must be closely examined in light of the suicide action. If the suicide intention is high and the lethality of the attempt was high, the risk for another serious suicide attempt or successful completion is also high (Bonner, 2001) Hospitalization would seem indicated. If the attempt was low to moderate in suicide intention (e.g., an act done in front of the staff) and the lethality was moderate to low (e.g., cutting), routine outpatient, M.A.P. interventions would seem indicated.

For some inmates with high suicide intention, a high level of attempt lethality, and an underlying mental illness resistant to treatment, consideration for the use of electroconvulsive therapy may be warranted (Guttmacher, 1994; Salzman, 1999). This treatment can provide significant relief to mental and mood suffering which has not responded to other forms of treatment. The potential benefits must especially be considered if the inmate is at high risk for eventual suicide.

Staff Monitoring and Housing

It should be obvious for Stage 4 of suicide action that a constant staff observation suicide watch in a therapeutic cell is indicated. In the event the inmate continues to exhibit suicide action on watch (e.g., head banging), consideration for the use of restraints and/or a head helmet to control the inmate is indicated. Once the inmate is out of crisis, his or her affective symptoms have improved, and he or she is willing to engage in a pro-living treatment plan, interventions can revert back to Stage 3. The inmate can be placed back in general population, housed with other inmates, and monitored by staff at fifteen-minute intervals. However, staff should remember that most suicide actions occur when an inmate appears to be improving and has regained some energy. Regular monitoring by mental health staff is critical at least until the inmate completely exits the suicide process, has hope, reasons for living, and purpose in living, and is no longer in emotional pain. As this occurs, interventions can return to Stage 2 and Stage 1, with the inmate being returned to general population and routine staff monitoring.

To help illustrate the practical application of these process interventions for the inmate involved in the suicide process, four case vignettes will now be presented with a proposed intervention plan for each.

Case Vignettes

Case (Stage 1): Inmate X strikes up a conversation with his housing unit officer. He tells the officer his wife just dumped him and that she was all he had on the outside. In a joking manner, Inmate X comments, "She probably wouldn't care if I hung up!"

Response: The correctional officer continues talking with Inmate X about how difficult it can be losing a relationship. The officer then asks Inmate X if he is thinking about suicide. Inmate X laughs and says, "Yeah just for a minute...but I would never do it. Got my kids...gonna get out of this place and be a father to them..." The officer asks Inmate X if he would like to talk to one of the mental health counselors. Inmate X says, "Not really...got my homeboy here...his old lady dumped him too...we kick it." The officer suggests to Inmate X that if he feels worse or believes he needs to speak with someone, please inform a staff member so they can get him hooked up with a counselor. Inmate X responds, "No problem...I'll be okay...thanks." The officer contacts mental health staff to discuss the case. The inmate has no history of the suicide process, nor does he come from one of the high-risk groups. The mental health counselor compliments the officer on his concern and professional handling of Inmate X. No further follow-up is needed and the inmate will remain in general population with his peers.

Case (Stage 2): Inmate X returns to his housing unit after seeing the parole board. He appears very uptight and upset, and the unit officer asks him what happened. The inmate angrily says, "Parole board screwed me over for the last time...not gonna do any more time...hit me till 2010...can't take anymore of this place!"

Response: The officer asks Inmate X if he is thinking about killing himself. X responds, "Seems the only way out of here." The officer tells the inmate he understands how he feels but does not think suicide is the way out. He tells Inmate X that he is sorry about what he is going through and would like to get him to speak to a counselor about this situation. Inmate X says, "No problem…can't see what they can do for me…unless they got power with the parole board." The officer calls mental health staff with the inmate in his presence. They tell him to send the inmate over. A mental health counselor then interviews Inmate X. He has no history of the suicide process and denies having a plan of suicide at the moment. The counselor suggests they set up an intervention plan that rationally examines the costs and benefits of suicide. In addition, the counselor asks the inmate to examine the magnitude of the problem, brainstorm possible solutions to the problem, and consider his reasons for living and his reasons for dying. The inmate agrees to take and read the book *Suicide: The Forever Decision*. He continues to see the counselor until he determines suicide is not a solution but would in fact cause trauma and emotional suffering for his children and mother, whom he loves very much. Inmate X then puts his energy in programming, keeping close ties with his loved ones, and preparing for the next parole board hearing in two years. All along the inmate remains in general population with other inmates and is monitored only routinely by staff.

Case (Stage 3): Inmate X arrives intoxicated at a county jail after being arrested for a DUI. The officer conducting the intake screening notices the inmate seems depressed and withdrawn, as well as intoxicated. The inmate will not answer the officer's questions. The officer, from his training, knows that this inmate comes from populations at risk, including first arrest for DUI, and intoxication. The inmate's affective state is depression and his controls to regulate his mood and behavior are poor by way of his intoxication.

Response: Inmate X will be placed on suicide watch with constant staff monitoring. Medical staff will examine the inmate and appropriate detoxification procedures will be implemented if indicated. Once the inmate is sober, stable, and able to engage in meaningful conversation, crisis intervention will be provided to help the inmate cope with the stress and embarrassment of his arrest. Accessing a family contact, if available, will be helpful as well as contact with an attorney to assist him in understanding his charges and what he should expect. Once it is determined the inmate is not in the suicide process and his mental state is stable, he should be placed in general population with other inmates. If there were any forms of suicide contemplation, cognitive interventions via books and/or staff would be indicated, as well as social support access and building. Going forward, only routine staff monitoring would be needed.

Case (Stage 4): Segregated Inmate X is found with a sheet tied around both his neck and a showerhead. It is unclear if the inmate is actually suspended or if he is just standing there.

Response: The responding officer calls for back up staff and medical assistance, and then enters the cell. The inmate's feet are off the ground, and the officer, along with arriving officers, supports and lifts the inmate and cuts the noose. They then hold the inmate while lowering him to the floor, protecting the head. The officer checks for breathing and pulse, both of which are present. The inmate is conscious. He opens his eyes and yells out, "I must die to defeat Satan and all of you demons from the fires of hell!" The staff knows this inmate to be mentally ill with a history of psychosis and suicide attempts. The inmate is carried on a stretcher to the medical department. A search of his cell turns up a number of pills hidden under his mattress, which are identified as Haldol tablets, an antipsychotic medication.

Once medically examined and stabilized, the inmate is placed on suicide watch under constant staff observation. The inmate is then examined by the on-duty mental health clinician who finds him to be actively psychotic. Suicide is a major theme of his delusional system to rid the world of Satan and demons. He has not been taking his antipsychotic medication and is currently unable and unwilling to give his consent for medication and treatment. Inmate X is in need of psychiatric hospitalization and authorization from a court for involuntary, psychiatric treatment. Once this occurs and the inmate is again stabilized on his medication, he may return to the correctional facility. He will require close monitoring by mental health staff, especially for medication compliance. Correctional staff will also need to promptly report any deterioration to mental health in order to prevent another psychotic episode and possible suicide attempt. Placing this inmate in segregation is contraindicated due to its association with mental breakdown unless one of the following conditions is met: he has become a danger to others, he is waiting for psychiatric hospitalization, or he is closely monitored by staff at fifteen-minute intervals.

Some General Intervention Considerations

In summarizing process interventions for suicidal inmates, several overriding issues are important to consider.

Segregation

Most suicide victims in jails and prisons were housed in conditions of isolation and sensory deprivation at the time of their death (Bonner, 2006a, 2005c, 2000, 1992a, 1992b; Hayes, 2004, 1995; Hayes & Rowan, 1988; Hayes & Kajdin, 1981). Common names for these places of isolation are the Drunk Tank, Bull Pen, Seclusion, Segregation, Administrative Detention, Disciplinary Segregation, Protective Custody, Special Housing Unit, and Restricted Housing Unit. Regardless of the name, inmates identify these places as the "Hole." While these units are designed to enhance security and control dangerous inmates, many of their residents are there for non-violent reasons such as intoxication, victimization, protective custody, minor institutional infractions, mental illness, administrative reviews for classification, and unavailable general population bed space.

Research (Bonner, 2006a 2005c, 1992a) and the courts (O'Leary, 1989) have concluded that placement of inmates in conditions of isolation and sensory deprivation can lead to depression, mental breakdown, and a morbid state of mind, which can be considered the direct cause of an inmate's suicide. If corrections is serious about inmate mental health care and suicide prevention, it must carefully reevaluate the use of segregation to manage inmates, particularly for those who do not pose a danger to others and who suffer from emotional upset, depression, problems of living, and mental illness. Special attention must be paid to anyone who's been involved in the suicide process.

Manipulation

Many inmates who threaten or gesture by self-mutilation are viewed as manipulators (Bonner, 2002). In other words, these inmates are thought to engage in these behaviors to compel staff or the institution to do something to meet their needs or wants. Staff dealing with these inmates often feel used and taken advantage of, and over time may react defensively by verbal attacks at worst and simple avoidance at best. Ironically, this staff response often reinforces the inmate self-harming behavior, so that he or she increases or intensifies the behavior to draw staff's attention further or punish staff for their lack of response.

Another tactic in dealing with these inmates is a problem solving, process approach (Clum & Febbraro, 2004; Rich & Bonner, 2004) which views the threats and gestures as an effort to solve some problem that couldn't be solved through other efforts. With this approach, staff help the inmate define the problem behind his or her behavior, understand the motives and intentions for the self-harm behavior, and brainstorm what other solution responses have not already been considered or tried.

If the problem is situational, the inmate's intention not suicide, and the motive is to arrive at a specific solution (e.g., transfer, cellmate change, avoidance of disciplinary sanctions), correctional counseling can be helpful. In this process, the correctional counselor can help the inmate by focusing on the negative consequences of self-harm behavior and brainstorm all possible alternative behaviors that might provide relief and solve the problem at hand. The inmate needs to learn that there are other options to improve and perhaps resolve the current problem. In addition, the inmate needs to learn that threats and gestures of self-harm may create additional problems. He must be informed that continuing such actions may result in control by staff through increased monitoring, property and privilege restriction, and if necessary, the use of correctional restraints.

Help Only if You Want It

As far as interventions go, it must be understood that the suicidal inmate cannot be helped unless others know about it—through behavior, mood, communications, or history. For the inmate who successfully conceals the suicide process, it is sometimes impossible to intervene as even our best intervention and assessment techniques do *not* read minds (Bonner, 2001). Our duty is to respond and intervene when an inmate shows signs, symptoms, or behaviors consistent with the suicide process, mental illness, hopelessness, and/or psychache. Fortunately, inmates will generally demonstrate to others that they are in crisis and contemplating suicide, namely because they are ambivalent about wanting to die and desperately seek solutions to their problems. If given the opportunity, they may even open up to staff and the mental health counselor and share their life story and reasons for contemplating suicide.

Relationship

No matter how well developed or sophisticated a suicide prevention program may be, its success will fundamentally depend on the relationship staff develop with the suicidal inmate (Bonner, 2005b, 1989). Indeed, the suicide stages in their various forms are most often a cry for help to others for problem solving and obtaining psychache relief. A staff-inmate relationship buffers the inmate from the ill effects of stress and problems in living, fosters trust and hope for relief, and in time will lead the suicidal inmate to new problem-solving alternatives, reasons for living, and hope for tomorrow. Only the element of genuine care and human compassion initiates and energizes the various process interventions to affect change in the suicidal person. The "good cop" personifies these qualities, as does the "good corrective worker."

Hope Builders

As discussed previously, the suicide process is fueled by a hopeless state of mind. It is this core mind state which must change to reverse and exit the suicide process. More often, the therapeutic relationship itself will build hope for the suicidal inmate. Faith based and family oriented programs can be particularly helpful in building life purpose and hope and enhancing reasons for living.

In conclusion, "the ultimate challenge for correctional suicide preventionists will be to assist at-risk and hopeless inmates to develop internal programs of purpose and hope, in often seemingly hopeless circumstances. Equally important, our work must advocate for a justice system in the new millennium that restores reasonable justice for the offender with real-life opportunities to correct oneself and work toward a better future when possible" (Bonner, 2000; p. 375).

6

Correctional Suicide Prevention Programs

As has been noted in previous chapters, inmate suicide is viewed as a process of stages, with multiple risk modalities, events, coping transactions, and behavioral responses leading up to the suicide act. Based on this model and the research of others (Hayes, 1995), correctional suicide prevention programs should have six core components: intake risk screening/assessment, housing, levels of supervision, process interventions, administrative review, and staff training. Professional program standards have evolved to guide correctional facilities in the development and implementation of effective suicide prevention programs.

The American Correctional Association (ACA, 2004) has issued a mandatory suicide prevention standard:

A suicide-prevention program is approved by the health authority and reviewed by the facility or program administrator. It includes specific procedures for handling intake, screening, identifying, and supervising of a suicide-prone inmate and is signed and reviewed annually. The program includes staff and inmate critical debriefing that covers the management of suicidal incidents, suicide watch, and death of an inmate or staff member. It ensures a review of critical incidents by administration, security, and health services. All staff with responsibility for inmate supervision are trained on an annual basis in the implementation of the program.

Training includes but is not limited to:

- Identifying the warning signs and symptoms of impending suicidal behavior

- Understanding the demographic and cultural parameters of suicidal behavior, including incidence and variations in precipitating factors

- Responding to suicidal and depressed inmates

- Communicating between correctional and health care personnel

- Using referral procedures-housing observation and suicide-watch level procedures

- Follow-up monitoring of inmates who make a suicide attempt(4-ALDF-4C-32). Reprinted by permission from the *Performance-Based Standards for Adult Local Detention Facilities, 4th Edition,* American Correctional Association, 2004.

The National Commission on Correctional Health Care standard has provided greater detail and more staff responsibilities in suicide prevention (NCCHC, 2003). Specifically, the standard reads, "The facility has a program that identifies and responds to suicidal inmates."

The discussion of the standard reads as follows:

The standard is intended to ensure that suicides are prevented if at all possible. When suicides do occur, appropriate corrective action is identified and implemented to prevent recurrences. While inmates may become suicidal at any point during their stay, high risk periods include the time immediately upon admission to a facility, following new legal problems (e.g., new charges, additional sentences, institutional proceedings, denial of parole), after the receipt of bad news regarding self or family (e.g., serious illness, the loss of a loved one), and after suffering some type of humiliation (e.g., sexual assault) or rejection. Inmates in specialized single-celled housing are also at increased risk of suicide. In addition, inmates who are in the early stages of recovery from severe depression may be at risk.

Key components of a successful suicide prevention include the following:

1. *Training.* All staff members who work with inmates are trained to recognize verbal and behavioral cues that indicate potential suicide, and how to respond appropriately. Initial and at least biennial training are provided, although annual training is highly recommended.

2. *Identification.* The receiving screening form contains observation and interview items related to the inmate's potential suicide risk. If a staff member identifies someone who is potentially suicidal, the inmate is placed on suicide precautions and is referred immediately to mental health staff.

3. *Referral.* There are procedures for referring potentially suicidal inmates and those who have attempted suicide to mental health care providers or facilities. The procedures specify a time frame for response to the referral.

4. *Evaluation.* An evaluation, conducted by a qualified mental health professional, designates the individual's level of suicide risk, level of supervision needed, and need for transfer to an inpatient mental health facility or program. Patients are reassessed regularly to identify any change in condition indicating a need for a change in supervision level or required transfer or commitment. The evaluation includes procedures for periodic follow-up assessment after the individual's discharge from suicide precautions.

5. *Housing.* Unless constant supervision is maintained, a suicidal inmate is not isolated. Rather, he or she is housed in general population, mental health unit, or medical infirmary, and close proximity to staff. All cells or rooms housing suicidal inmates are as suicide-resistant as possible (e.g., without protrusions of any kind that would enable the inmate to hang himself or herself.)

6. *Monitoring.* There are procedures for monitoring an inmate who has been identified as potentially suicidal. Regular, documented supervision is maintained, usually every fifteen minutes or more frequently if necessary. While there are several protocols for monitoring suicidal inmates, when any actively suicidal inmate is housed alone in a room, supervision through continuous monitoring by staff should be maintained. Other supervision aids (e.g., closed circuit television, inmate companions, or watchers) can be used as a supplement to, but never as a substitute for, staff monitoring.

7. *Communication.* Procedures for communication between health care and correctional personnel regarding the status of the inmate are in place to provide clear and current information. These procedures also include communication between transferring authorities (e.g., county facility, medical/psychiatric facility) and facility correctional personnel.

8. *Intervention.* There are procedures addressing how to handle a suicide attempt in progress, including appropriate first-aid measures.

9. *Notification.* Procedures are in place stating when correctional administrators, outside authorities, and family members are notified of potential, attempted, or completed suicides.

10. *Reporting.* Procedures for documenting the identification and monitoring of potential or attempted suicides are detailed, as are procedures for reporting a completed suicide.

11. *Review.* There are procedures for medical and administrative review if a suicide or a serious suicide attempt (as defined by the suicide plan) occurs. See P-A-10 Procedure in the Event of an Inmate Death for details on these processes.

12. *Critical incident debriefing.* The facility specifies the procedures for offering timely critical incident debriefing to all affected personnel and inmates. Critical incident debriefing is a process whereby individuals are provided an opportunity to express their thoughts and feelings about a critical incident (e.g., suicide attempt, suicide), develop an understanding of critical stress symptoms, and develop ways of dealing with those symptoms.

(P-G-05 Essential)-Reprinted by permission from the *2003 Standards for Health Services in Prisons*, National Commission on Correctional Health Care, Chicago, IL.

Lindsay Hayes (2005a) most recently published *A Practitioner's Guide to Developing a Sound Suicide Prevention Program.* This outstanding work should be in the library of all correctional practitioners who are involved in suicide prevention programming. It covers guiding principles to suicide prevention, critical aspects of suicide prevention policy, and a sample suicide prevention policy with attachments. As highlighted earlier in Table 4-1, this guide provides specific assessment tools to screen and assess inmate suicide risk. A two-level inmate supervision protocol of close observation and constant observation is recommended.

Specifically, according to Hayes (2005a): "*Close Observation* is reserved for the inmate who is not actively suicidal, but expresses suicidal ideation (e.g., expressing a wish to die without a specific threat or plan) or has a recent prior history of self-destructive behavior. In addition, an inmate who denies suicidal ideation or does not threaten suicide, but demonstrates other concerning behavior (through actions, current circumstances, or recent history) indicating the potential for self-injury, should be placed under close observation. Staff should observe such an inmate at staggered intervals not to exceed every fifteen minutes (e.g., five, ten, seven minutes, etc). *Constant observation* is reserved for the inmate who is actively suicidal, either threatening or engaging in suicidal behavior. Staff should observe such an inmate on a continuous, uninterrupted basis" (p. 7).

The area of suicide prevention training has not yet been addressed and is considered the foundation of an effective program. A program is only as good as the knowledge, skills, and attitudes demonstrated by correctional staff. All correctional staff responsible for inmate supervision should be trained in all aspects of the institution's suicide prevention program. Correctional officers in particular interact more with inmates that any other staff; observing, supervising, and communicating with inmates twenty-four hours a day, seven days a week. Officers get to know inmates, their dispositions, life situations, stressors, behavior, and mood changes and are most likely to come across the inmate who is having problems, in crisis, and/or showing signs of suicide risk (Bonner, 1992b). Three key elements of training have been identified: risk identification, interventions, and attitude. The first two areas have been covered in previous chapters. Suffice to say, all correctional staff should know how to screen an inmate for suicide risk and be able to identify triggers, high-risk periods, high-risk places, and the process nature of inmate suicide, then make appropriate referrals for assessment and intervention.

An interpersonal, humanistic, problem-solving attitude of all correctional staff is considered the most important element for effective suicide prevention programs (Bonner, 1992b). Correctional workers are tasked with the care, custody, and security of offenders. The care aspect has to do with taking care of and responding to inmates who present a variety of personal problems, to include mental health concerns. They are responsible for preventing suicides when inmates demonstrate observable or verbal signs consistent with suicide risk. Identifying, communicating, solving problems, and referring inmates are important components of inmate care. Training should emphasize this philosophy, teach communication and problem-solving skills with inmates in crisis, and dispute detrimental attitudes to and myths of suicide prevention. Authoritarian, macho-cop, we vs. they, and punitive characteristics of correctional staff undermine suicide prevention and create an atmosphere ripe for suicides, disturbances, violence, and liability (Bonner 2005a, 1992b).

Role-playing, value clarification exercises, and reviewing the Code of Conduct and Ethical Principles of Correctional Workers are all important in this regard. Sound personnel selection procedures should be in place to weed out applicants with these destructive attitudes. Correctional workers should also be familiar with the common, stereotypic myths associated with inmate suicide that lead to fear, misunderstanding, and unresponsiveness. Some of the common inmate suicide myths are: (1) suicidal inmates really want to die so there is nothing you can do to stop them, (2) suicidal inmates are crazy and dangerous, and (3) talking about suicide with inmates will put the idea in their heads and make them suicidal.

Inmate suicidal behavior should be normalized in training so that employees come to see suicide as a desperate attempt to escape unbearable problems of living and emotional suffering. A number of small group discussion exercises can be held in this regard.

Fortunately, several excellent training resources exist for correctional suicide prevention training. Rowan and Hayes (1988) have developed a very comprehensive training manual that comprehensively addresses identification, intervention, and interpersonal attitude, and provides numerous handouts, exercises, and overhead transparencies. Hayes (2005b) is currently updating and revising this manual, and it should prove to be the state of the art training standard for correctional systems to follow. In addition, the *New York Local Forensic Suicide Prevention Crisis Service Model* (Sovoronsky & Shapiro, 1989) entails a comprehensive, 8-hour, structured training program to be completed annually by all correctional staff. This program provides an objective, knowledge/skills/attitude test to ensure staff has adequately mastered these areas. In addition, the American Correctional Association (1991) has developed a self-study program in correctional suicide prevention that also includes a test for certification. Finally, the National Center for Institutions and Alternatives frequently and critically reviews training programs and can provide invaluable guidance in developing and implementing a training program for each correctional institution.

The National Center for Institutions and Alternatives under the direction of Lindsay Hayes also frequently reviews model suicide prevention programs in the publication *Jail Suicide/Mental Health Update*. This publication is an invaluable resource for institutions and correctional and mental health care staff (See Chapter 9-Resources). New York State, for example, has a well known model suicide prevention program that is considered one of the most comprehensive programs available. It features an eight-hour training program for all staff, a mental health resource manual, detailed policy and procedural guidelines, and specific suicide prevention intake screening guidelines (Sovornski & Shapiro, 1989).

Pennsylvania's Department of Corrections has also developed an outstanding state of the art suicide prevention program, which has received rave reviews. (Couturier & Maue, 2000). Some of its past innovative actions have included:

1.   Developing a Suicide Risk Indicator Checklist for SMU/RMU (segregation)

2.   Expanding mental health services

3.   Diverting mentally ill inmates from segregation

4. Monitoring suicidal inmates via an automated tracking system

5. Expanding correctional officer training to include an 8-hour program for new employees and a two-hour training refresher course annually for all employees

6. Developing a suicide prevention brochure to be given to all inmates

7. Developing a suicide prevention videotape for all inmates to see

8. Increasing the frequency and thoroughness of internal reviews for any suicide attempt or completion

9. Mandating suicide smocks and blankets for all suicide watches

10. Enhancing mental health services for lifers and long term offenders

11. Mandating the use of emergency rescue tools in all facilities

12. Mandating critical stress debriefings and defusion for all staff and inmates involved in fatal events.

Program outcome research has shown that inmate suicide rates decrease substantially when these programs are implemented. (Cox, Landberg, & Pravati, 1989; Couturier & Maue, 2000; Rowan & Hayes, 1988; White & Schimmel, 1995.) Such programs are also an institution's primary legal defense in the event of an inmate's suicide (Cohen, 1992; Danto, 1997; Robertson, 2004). Regrettably, the majority of Department of Corrections surveyed by Hayes (1995, 2004b) did not have suicide prevention programs to cover the six key components of an effective suicide prevention program.

7

Liability and Risk Management

While suicide behind bars is a process with usually detectable stages, behaviors, and modality risk factors, an inmate will occasionally go to great lengths to conceal his or her suicide intention to ensure he or she is not stopped. In such cases, where an inmate is absolutely intent on dying, there sometimes may be little an institution can do to prevent the suicide from occurring. Correctional and mental health workers are not held to a standard of a crystal ball (O'Leary, 1989) but are only able and responsible to take reasonable action to prevent a suicide when an inmate exhibits the known risk factors. Nonetheless, when an inmate suicide does occur, it is in the best interest of the institution and its staff to conduct an official investigation into the actions that led to the inmate's death (Spellman & Heyne, 1989). In addition, this investigation should include a "psychological autopsy" to try to identify the inmate's intent to die and the various life events and psychological processes that resulted in the suicide.

Sanchez (1999) has covered this process in detail and recommends the psychological autopsy cover the following areas: Incident, autopsy/toxicology findings, background information, mental health history, medical history, institutional functioning, personality dynamics, precipitating events, pre-suicidal functioning, and motive for suicide, summary/conclusions, and recommendations.

This effort is useful to employees in helping them understand what contributed to the inmate's suicide, determine if policy or operating procedures might be modified in such a way that would have reduced the risk, and provide a comprehensive, investigative document which may become critical in the event there is a law suit.

In terms of litigation regarding inmate suicides, a review of much of the case law is confusing and often contradictory (Lee, 2002). Most cases end up in out of court settlements. Civil right actions, the most hard to prove, require that correctional staff had specific knowledge that there was a strong likelihood an inmate was suicidal and took no reasonable action to prevent the suicide from occurring. These cases can provide injunctive relief and compensatory and punitive damages. The legal proof of deliberate indifference was stringently defined by the famous Supreme Court Farmer vs. Brennan Case (Hayes, 1999). Issued in 1994, the Court stated: "We hold that a prison official cannot be held liable for denying humane conditions of confinement unless the official knows of and disregards an excessive risk to inmate health or safety, the official must both be aware of facts from which the inference is drawn that a substantial risk of serious harm exists, and he must also draw the inference." (p. 837, cited in Hayes, 1999)

According to Hayes (1999), correctional officials can be deliberately indifferent when: (1) an inmate threatened or attempted suicide, (2) the threat/attempt was known to staff, and (3) sufficient efforts were not made to protect the inmate from harm. Robertson (2004) suggested the Supreme Court's interpretation of deliberate indifference was comparable to criminal recklessness, setting the constitutional bar extremely low, and making it almost impossible to obtain relief in civil right actions regarding an inmate's suicide.

Tort suits, on the other hand, seek damages only as the result of negligence that caused or failed to prevent a suicide (Hayes, 1995). These cases are much easier to prove and are most representative of inmate suicide litigation. Negligence has been found for a number of inmate suicide issues, including an institution's poor track record of suicides; poor conditions of confinement (including placing an inmate in segregation); failure to identify at-risk inmates who present well known suicide risk factors such as intoxication, physical impairments, mental illness, suicide statements and acts; previous suicide attempts or morbid states of mind; placement of juveniles in adult correctional facilities; and suicide risk profiles (O'Leary, 1989).

In addition, liability in inmate suicides has been established in custodial actions, or lack thereof, for inadequate institutional or staffing capacity to respond to the problem, inadequate policies and procedures, lack of staff training, poor physical structure, lack of medical referrals or treatment, inadequate supervision, inadequate search, isolation, and infrequent monitoring. Greater weight in liability has been placed on detoxification facilities for suicide risk and prevention, suicide risk screening in jails, and long-term mental health treatment in prisons (O'Leary, 1989).

Other successfully litigated areas have included failure to foresee suicide, inadequate organization and staffing of mental health services, failure of medical staff to properly diagnose and treat suicidal inmates, failure to examine prior mental health/suicide records, poor facility design, inadequate record keeping, failure to share information between custody and mental health staff, failure to follow suicide prevention policies, and failure of staff to carry out their respective responsibilities in an institution's suicide prevention program (Hayes, 1995). For a thorough review of suicide negligence case law, the reader is referred to comprehensive law reviews by Lee (2002), Hayes (1995), O'Leary (1989), and Robertson (2004).

In terms of risk management and reducing liability, as cited earlier, professional standards have been developed to guide the correctional agency in providing effective, ethically and legally sound suicide prevention programs. These standards serve as a benchmark reference for courts in their decision-making. Institutions that have well-written suicide prevention policies to cover the key areas of risk screening/assessment, housing, levels of supervision, process interventions for the suicidal inmate, administrative reviews, and staff training, and implement these policies accordingly are doing an excellent job at managing risk and will be well prepared in the unfortunate event a suicide does occur and a law suit is filed.

1. Special risk management considerations must be made for mental health care professionals who have a critical role and a high stake in inmate suicide prevention. These specialized staff members are tasked with rendering opinions about risk level, providing recommendations about suicide precautions and levels of staff monitoring, and implementing appropriate therapeutic interventions to reduce suicidality. Successful suicide malpractice claims generally fall into the following categories: (1) Failure to diagnose and safeguard, (2) Failure to recognize a patient's suicide tendencies and not take precautionary measures to protect the patient, and (3) Failure to use proper care and treatment. (Jones & Berman, 1993, p. 92)

To provide good care to the suicidal inmate, the mental health clinician needs to know exactly the clinical and legal standards of care involved in working with suicidal people. All clinicians should have in their library Bruce Bongar's (1992) *The Suicidal Patient: Clinical and Legal Standards of Care*. This is the state of the art, classic text in suicide risk management. Correctional mental health professionals should also regularly attend advanced training in working with suicidal patients, as most graduate training programs do not adequately cover this specialized area.

The American Association of Suicidology is the national professional organization dedicated to research, prevention, and education in suicide. All correctional mental health clinicians should belong to this organization that sponsors

regular continuing education training programs, a peer-reviewed scholarly journal, crisis center certification, suicide survivor support services, and annual professional conferences. It is also highly recommended that clinicians carry
adequate levels of liability insurance (i.e., $3,000,000 per claim), as well as their
correctional work site coverage. While staff assume protection if practicing within
the scope of their job duties, this is not a guarantee and clinicians can be sued in
their independent practice under their license or certification.

Mental health clinicians should also be especially cautious of ethical compro-
mises in correctional health care that interferes with their professional role and
the provision of adequate mental health treatment and suicide prevention services
(Bonner & VandeCreek, 2006). Clinicians should bring such issues to the attention of their supervisors and, if not resolved, to their respective professional asso-
ciations, the American Correctional Health Services Association, the American
Association for Correctional and Forensic Psychology, and if necessary the gov-
ernmental body responsible for correctional mental health care funding. Other-
wise, correctional mental health providers will not only find themselves on shaky
ethical ground, but may also be held legally to a standard of care they cannot provide due to the limitations placed upon them by their employing agencies.

To assist clinicians in risk management, the model of B.E. S.M.A.R.T. (Bonner, 2005b) is reviewed below:

Blindness is a critical psychological factor for assessment, intervention, and
risk management for the suicidal inmate. The suicidal inmate's mind is dark and
blind to alternative solutions, coping responses, problem solutions, reasons for
living, and hope. This darkness/blindness varies in degree depending upon the
inmate's mental state for suicide, affective state and psychache threshold, and
psychosocialbiological history context. In intervening with the suicidal inmate,
the clinician must determine the appropriate interventions and necessary precautions for the inmate's level of psychological darkness or blindness. The record
should reflect this assessment and the rationale for selected interventions and precautions.

Empathy is a core theme of the therapeutic relationship with the suicidal
inmate. It must guide the therapist in decision-making and treatment planning.
The record should reflect this understanding and how suicide has come to make
experiential sense for the inmate. Risk level estimation should be made for the
short-term depending upon the inmate's mental and affective states, and the particular stage of the suicide process he or she currently experiences. Good inmate/
patient care and good risk management direct the mental health clinician to use
as many data sources as available to develop this understanding, and to include

reviews of previous records and interviews with correctional staff, family members, and inmate peers. The record should reflect these efforts and the data obtained.

Another important, yet intentionally forgotten, aspect of empathy in inmate risk management is the extension of this understanding and compassion to family and significant others of the suicidal inmate. As much as the inmate allows, these significant attachments can be an integral part of the treatment plan. In the event the inmate does commit suicide, the therapist should expand, but not retreat, from this relationship, by providing outreach and sympathy to the grieving family. When possible, the clinician should educate loved ones about the survivor grief reaction and encourage them to seek counseling services and participate in suicide survivor support groups. The American Association of Suicidology can be contacted for a national listing of such support services. This outreach goes a long way in preventing malpractice claims, which often come about because of the family's anger and alienation from the system and the victim's health care provider.

The Stage of the suicide process is critically important in risk management. Determining how far an inmate has progressed in the suicide process will determine the level of process interventions and suicide precautions and the need for hospitalization. The inmate's history in the suicide stages is also very important in decision-making. The more the inmate has moved through the suicide process, the greater the stage, suicide intention, and planning, and the weaker the emotional controls, the greater the risk is for eventual suicide. The record should reflect this assessment currently and historically for the suicidal inmate. As noted earlier, there are structured, standardized instruments to help the clinician in measuring these stages and making an estimation of suicide risk. Generally, outpatient psychotherapy is most appropriate for inmates at the stages of passive suicide ideation, suicide contemplation, and suicide planning and decision-making (as long as the inmate's controls are intact and he or she is willing and able to enter into a pro-living relationship agreement with safety nets established). In addition, rapid employment of treatment interventions at Stage 3 to reduce emotional suffering and fortify controls is necessary. For the inmate at the psychache threshold, especially with a history of previous dyscontrol and suicide actions, the staff will need to place the inmate on constant suicide watch with consideration for inpatient, psychiatric treatment.

The record should note the suicide stage, the history of the stage progression, and the suicidal inmate's level of controls. Based on this assessment, appropriate stage-level process interventions should be provided, along with the documented rationale for these decisions. It should be noted that for inmates who are in need of interventions beyond the capability of the facility, the mental health clinician is responsible not only for the referral but insuring appropriate follow-up occurs. The clinician is also responsible for insuring administrative and correctional staff members are aware of this inmate's treatment needs and the level of staff supervision required until follow-up can occur. The record should reflect all of these actions to ensure there is no appearance of abandonment or miscommunication with all responsible staff.

Modality refers to the biopsychosocial systems operating in the suicidal inmate as he or she transacts with stress and problems of incarceration over time. The **M.A.P.** guide can help the clinician in assessing the most relevant systems in the suicidal inmate. It also provides a logical extension to treatment targets and the interventions proposed and implemented. The record should reflect what is being done, why it is being done, how it ties into the multimodal assessment, and the effectiveness of the interventions once implemented. In the event improvement is not seen, the therapist will want to modify the treatment plan and document in the record how and why additional interventions are being employed.

Alternatives: The mental health provider must recognize mental health interventions are one avenue among many that may help the inmate retreat from the suicide process. Other viable interventions might include increased family contact, medical examination to rule out physiological causes, social services, vocational training, pastoral/spiritual counseling, self-help programs, faith-based programs, and inmate-peer "buddy" social supports. The clinician should encourage all possibilities for emotional relief and document these avenues in the treatment record.

The intervention plan should also address a relapse prevention program to help the inmate prepare for future possible triggers, problems, and emotions that might activate the suicide process again. The clinician should make periodic check-ups on the inmate who has retreated from the suicide process, as the risk exists for a return to the process at some future point. This ongoing concern represents good therapeutic care and good risk management. The record, of course, should reflect these activities.

Risk level estimation is a constant process during the course of treatment. This estimation is based on the stage the inmate is in while incarcerated and the **M.A.P.** modalities operating in the inmate's coping transactions with incarceration stress over time. Risk level should be categorized as low, moderate, high, and imminent, which should then directly impact the treatment planning, suicide precautions, level of staff supervision, and safety networks. Inmates at Stage 1 of passive suicide ideation are likely to be assigned a low suicide risk and are often best housed in general population, without special staff supervision, and involved in outpatient counseling to deal with the problem at hand. Inmates at Stage 2 of suicide contemplation are assigned a low-moderate risk and also are usually best housed in general population without special supervision, as long as he or she is willing to engage in a problem-solving, cost-benefit counseling process. Inmates at Stage 3 who have made the decision to commit a planned suicide but who are willing to engage in a pro-living relationship with the mental health counselor are also best housed in general population, with closer staff monitoring such as every fifteen minutes. The inmate at Stage 3 who is unwilling to engage in a pro-living relationship agreement and/or whose emotional controls are weak due to intoxication, psychosis, or impulsivity, would be considered a high risk and should be placed in a therapeutic, safe room with constant staff watch. Immediate crisis stabilization, intensive suicide precautions, and possible hospitalization would be needed. The record should reflect all of these steps and the actions the therapist took to protect the inmate from suicide action.

Finally, **T**reatment refers to all the various interventions provided to target the multiple modalities and stages of the suicide process. The therapeutic relationship is the power source for the success of such interventions as it will instill hope and reasons for living in the midst of emotional pain and despair. A validating therapeutic relationship engages the suicidal inmate to try and trust these interventions to provide relief and reverse the suicide process. The field has advanced to the point that specific types of interventions have been demonstrated empirically to reduce suicidality and are considered the standard of care. Therapists will want to use cognitive therapy for the mental and affective states of the suicide process and dialectical-behavior therapy for the affective state and emotional regulation. Pharmacological interventions will also be important to relieve emotional suffering and increase the inmate's psychache threshold. The record should reflect this multimodal, multistage approach and the selected rationale for interventions.

In conclusion, the B.E. S.M.A.R.T. model offers a simplistic, multimodal, stage-level, data-based guide for the correctional mental health care provider in providing good relationship care, appropriate stage/modality-specific interventions, risk management, and documentation in working with the suicidal offender.

Note: The foregoing chapter and B.E. S.M.A.R.T. model were adapted in part from *A psychotherapist's dark journey into the suicidal mind: A relationship approach to understanding and healing* (pp. 56–62) by R. L. Bonner (2005b). Copyright by the iUniverse Press. Used with permission. The B.E. S.M.A.R.T. model is simply a working guide for the clinician in suicide risk management. Clinicians should receive regular professional training in suicide risk management, modify their efforts according to the unique biopsychosocial dynamics of each individual inmate, and always seek consultation when unsure or experiencing limited progress.

8

Controversial Issues in Correctional Suicide Prevention

Generally speaking, suicide prevention programs following ACA and NCCHC standards and providing the six core components (risk screening/assessment, housing, levels of supervision, process interventions, administrative reviews, and staff training) are considered clinically, ethically, and legally sound. When practices circumvent or stray from these guidelines, the methods at best are controversial and at worst legally indefensible. Lindsay Hayes (2003, 1997, 1995b) has provided a review of some of these problematic shortcuts:

No-Suicide Contracts

Some correctional facilities use boilerplate contracts for all inmates to sign upon admission, such as "I promise not to harm myself while at _____ jail/prison and will alert staff if I think I will harm myself." Mental health clinicians also frequently use verbal or written no-suicide contracts in working with suicidal people. These contracts are troublesome on several fronts. First, the contract is usually self-serving to the agency or clinician but really does not provide any meaningful legal protection. Second, such contracts assume an inmate has complete control over his or her suicidal impulses and psychache. Third and most importantly, these contracts are usually one-sided—stating what the inmate will do or not do—and do not reflect a meaningful, therapeutic relationship of validation and trust. The pro-living relationship agreement is designed to reflect a relationship of compassion and reasons for living, which are significantly meaningful for the suicidal inmate. However, it is not the contract that prevents suicide. It is the therapeutic relationship (Bonner, 2005b).

Stripping a Potentially Suicidal Inmate Naked and Putting Him in Isolation
Believe it or not, this practice does still continue and has been shared with this author on a number of occasions when conducting personnel interviews with applicants that work in county jails. Suffice to say, stripping a depressed or suicidal inmate naked is dehumanizing and most likely will make the inmate more depressed and suicidal. If the inmate is considered high risk for suicide, there are suicide-proof blankets and smocks that allow the inmate to maintain his dignity. It is absolutely unbelievable and disheartening to know, after all the research, litigation, and development of professional standards, that the practice of isolation continues. O'Leary (1989) summarized the court decisions best when he noted that placing an inmate in isolation/segregation can lead to a morbid state of mind, which legally has been found to be the direct cause of an inmate's suicide.

Don't Talk With Inmates
It is also amazing to this author during personnel interviews how many applicants and officers from other facilities believe "it is not my job...I'm no shrink...not gonna talk about an inmate's problems." This negative attitude creates an atmosphere that is ripe for inmate suicides as well as other crisis-oriented behaviors. Good correctional workers, like good police officers, are all about walking and talking and problem solving. This approach takes care of small problems, prevents bigger problems from occurring, can avert a suicide, and can prevent inmate problems from escalating to violence or disturbances. When a correctional worker sees or suspects an inmate is having personal trouble, it is his or her job to talk to the inmate, find out what is going on, look for suicide risk factors, offer encouragement and hope, and when indicated, make a referral to mental health staff.

Use of Inmates to Conduct Suicide Watch
Some correctional institutions use inmate companions or watchers to provide a formal, constant suicide watch of a suicidal inmate. The primary reason for this action is to save money in the hiring of staff, regardless what the documented rationale might say. If applying the process model of suicide-to-suicide watches, it would primarily be inmates at Stage 3 (suicide planning and decision-making with weak controls) and Stage 4 where a suicide attempt has occurred that would be placed on a constant suicide watch. Inmates at earlier stages would generally be better off in general population with close staff monitoring and getting counseling for the identified problem.

Given this model, it would seem to be a concern that inmates who have advanced this far in the suicide process are placed under the responsibility and watch of other inmates. According to the National Commission of Correctional Health Care (NCCHC, 2003): "…when any actively suicidal inmate is housed alone in a room, supervision through *continuous* monitoring by *staff* should be maintained. Other supervision aids (e.g., closed circuit television, inmate companions or watchers) can be used as a *supplement* to, but never as a substitute for, staff monitoring." (P-G-05, Suicide Prevention Program, Discussion No. 6).

The responsibility for inmate supervision, and most critically for an inmate who is actively suicidal, ethically and legally falls exclusively on staff (Bonner, 2005d).

Using Closed Circuit Television Monitoring to Conduct Suicide Watches

Inmate suicides have been known to occur while they're being monitored and taped by TV's. When TV monitoring is used, staff is frequently expected to observe all the feeds on all the available screens throughout an institution, in addition to conducting other duties. It is not uncommon for staff to experience monitor hypnosis, which distracts them from fully attending to what is displayed on the monitor. Reception can also be fuzzy or distorted. Experts suggest TV monitoring should be used only as a supplement to one-on-one staff-inmate supervision during a suicide watch.

Dealing with Manipulative Inmates

Correctional staff is accustomed to inmates playing games and trying to "get one over" on them or the system. Unfortunately, when it comes to suicide, the risks are too great to treat any suicidal behavior as manipulative or attention-seeking. It is simply safer to treat all suicide threats and behaviors as serious, ensuring proper staff supervision and mental health staff referral. Hayes (2001) noted that when suicidal inmates are viewed as manipulative, they are often ignored or placed in segregation. Often the inmate will then increase the self-harming behavior to get the attention that is purposely being withheld. In this process, accidental deaths may occur via an inmate's miscalculation or staff's avoidance/unresponsiveness. At the very least, it is in everyone's best interest to closely monitor the inmate and have him or her evaluated by a mental health clinician for suicide risk. In the event the clinician concludes an inmate is exhibiting self-harming behavior for reasons other than suicide or death (e.g., transfer, cell change, drug-seeking; etc.), the clinician will want to have a treatment plan to target these motives, behaviors, and ineffective problem-solving skills. Such individuals are still in need of close staff supervision until the behaviors and motives have been modified. Placing these inmates in segregation should be cautiously considered, as the isolation and infrequent staff interactions may only reinforce and escalate the self-harming behavior (Bonner, 2002).

Protecting the Crime Scene and the Presumption of Death

The first priorities when discovering a suicide attempt or completion is administering first aid, providing CPR (if warranted), and summoning medical staff to the emergency situation. All correctional staff should be regularly trained in these procedures and furnished with protective gear, a CPR pocket mask, latex gloves, and other appropriate infectious disease equipment. All staff are responsible for administering first aid and/or CPR until medical personnel arrive. Even if vital signs do not exist, staff members are to continue CPR in an attempt to reestablish vital signs and bring back a person to life. Along with this responsibility, staff should always approach a suicide event as a health emergency situation, and only then secondarily as a potential crime scene. Inmates who are found hanging should be immediately cut down by staff with an emergency rescue tool and be provided first aid and CPR. For inmates who have cut themselves, staff should use a barrier protection to apply pressure to the wound until medical personnel arrive.

9

Resources in Suicide Prevention Programming

These resources should not be considered as *official* endorsements from the publisher. The author has personally found many of these resources to be very helpful in working with suicidal offenders and developing effective suicide prevention programs. Readers are encouraged to research the field to determine the full array of current resources and services available in correctional suicide prevention.

Lindsay Hayes, Project Director
National Center for Institutions and Alternatives
40 Lantern Lane
Mansfield, MA 02048
1-508-337-8806
www.ncianet.org/cjjsl.cfm

National Commission on Correctional Health Care
1145 W. Diversey Pkwy.
Chicago, IL 60614
1-773-880-1460
E-mail info@ncchc.org
www.ncchc.org

American Association of Suicidology
5221 Wisconsin Avenue, N.W.
Washington, DC 20015
1-202-237-2280
www.suicidology.org

Paul Quinnett, Ph.D., President
QPR Institute-Suicide Prevention Training
P.O. Box 2867
Spokane, WA 99220
1-888-726-7926
www.qprinstitute.com

National Institute of Corrections
1860 Industrial Circle
Suite A
Longmont, CO 80501
1-800-877-1461
www.nicic.org

American Correctional Association
4380 Forbes Blvd.
Lanham, MD 20706-4322
1-800-222-5646
www.aca.org

Suicide Prevention/Crisis-Service Model
NY State Commission of Corrections
60 S. Pearl St.
Albany, NY 12207
1-518-474-1416

Lance Couturier, Ph.D.
Frederick R. Maue, M.D.
PA Department of Corrections
P.O. Box 598
Camp Hill, PA 17001
1-717-731-7301

American Jail Association
1000 Day Road
Suite 100
Hagerstown, MD 21740
1-301-790-3930
www.aja.org

American Association for Correctional and Forensic Psychology
John Gannon, Ph.D., President
Central Coast Consultancy
897 Oak Park Blvd, #124
Pismo, CA 93449
1-805-489-0665
www.aa4cfp.org

American Correctional Health Services Association
250 Gatsby Place
Alpharetta, GA 30022-6161
1-877-918-1842
www.achsa.org

Ferguson Products
303 Potrero, Suite #2
Santa Cruz, CA 95060
1-831-458-0223
www.preventsuicide.com
(suicide proof smocks and blankets)

10

Taking Care of Staff in Correctional Suicide Prevention

The National Commission on Correctional Health Care (2003) recognized staff members are at risk for suffering stress and trauma as the result of responding to suicide emergencies. "Critical Incident Stress Debriefing" is recommended for all staff involved with such incidents. Pennsylvania's Department of Corrections reinforced this recommendation by including it as a mandatory program for staff and inmates who knew or were involved with the victim. According to Hayes (1992), staff responding to suicide emergencies will often experience a set of psychological and physiological reactions—most of which are considered normal—and may appear at different stages:

1. During the incident, symptoms may include confusion, non-directed activity, disorientation, tunnel vision, crying, muscle tenseness (clenching teeth, etc.), profuse sweating, chest pain, and/or increased heart beat;

2. Post-incident symptoms may begin to appear within hours after the incident and include blurred vision, loss of memory, confusion, non-directed activity, disorientation, and restlessness;

3. Delayed post-incident stress symptoms may occur weeks or months after the incident and include restlessness, irritability, chronic fatigue, sleep disturbances, anxiety, depression, moodiness, muscle tremors, concentration difficulties, substance abuse, nightmares, headaches, vomiting, and suspiciousness. (pp. 10–11, cited in Hayes, 1992.)

In addition to the stress and anxiety associated with the suicide trauma, staff members also frequently suffer from the "Suicide Survivor Syndrome" which occurs in people who knew, worked with, or are related to the suicide victim. It is not unusual for survivors to obsessively question themselves on what they missed and why they didn't see the suicide coming. Often they blame themselves for the suicide and suffer long-term guilt. Strong support, encouragement, and occasionally professional counseling or survivor support groups will help the survivor eventually recover from this syndrome.

Survivors also need to hear and eventually integrate within themselves the fact that some suicides cannot be prevented—that when the victim does not show suicide risk signs or communicate his or her intention, not even the best of the mental health professionals can read minds or stop someone who has made up his or her mind to kill himself. As professionals and fellow human beings, we can sometimes only help the person who shows us through his or her behavior, communications, and/or history that he or she is in the suicide process with multimodal risk factors.

In addition to suffering critical incident and survivor stress, employees are often interrogated or targeted by correctional system administrators or reviewers, who attempt to explain a suicide and shift blame from an institution or system. While perhaps not a popular sentiment in the corrections field, it has been this author's experience that we do a pretty good job of finger-pointing and "Monday morning quarterbacking" when bad things happen (most of which are out of our control). For the many good staff that care about inmates and take their jobs seriously, this reaction can be deeply hurtful. Perhaps this is why I vividly remember my last inmate suicide, ten years ago, where I, along with some wonderful human beings and professional correctional workers, ultimately felt we'd entered the cell and personally hung the inmate in question. This painful lesson increased our survivor trauma and for many of us sensitized us to what a mean-spirited business this can sometimes be.

Given these multiple stress and trauma factors, coupled with the high stress nature of correctional work in general (Cornelius, 1994), employees can be at risk for a number of physical and emotional disorders that can also lead to suicide if not abated. While the situation is given virtually no attention, correctional workers such as police officers (Loo, 2003) suffer greatly from depression, anxiety, cardiovascular disease, alcohol abuse, and relationship breakups. Such difficulties can lead a person to despair, hopelessness, and psychache, which too will fuel the suicide process. Rather than ignoring or minimizing this issue, corrections would do well to openly acknowledge this hazard of the job and provide employees opportunities to discuss, educate, and access professional counseling and treatment. Staff members should be on the lookout for these risk factors in themselves, their fellow employees, and family members and take proactive steps to relieve suffering and reverse the suicide process. Good correctional workers care deeply about each other and the inmates under their supervision.

11

The Conclusion of Suicide as a Process behind Bars

The problem of suicidal behavior behind bars is a serious one that has fortunately been attracting a great deal of attention in recent years. We now have a good idea of its frequency and the common risk factors. We also know there are unique characteristics about jail, prison, and juvenile detention populations that increase the risk for suicidal behavior.

The common denominator for most correctional suicides is housing in isolation or segregation. Research has shown these conditions worsen emotional suffering and can create an isolation panic that may plunge an inmate into suicide action. Unfortunately, in spite of the research, the use of segregation continues to be a common correctional practice in managing offenders, many of whom have been placed there for non-violent reasons. Suicidal behavior is rarely, if ever, an isolated event. It is a culmination of stages, biopsychosocial risk factors, and stress and coping failures, and it is fueled by a hopeless state of mind.

Correctional workers are responsible for the identification of and communication with inmates who demonstrate risk for suicide. They are also responsible for referring such inmates to mental health services for a formal risk assessment to determine the degree of suicide risk and the required levels of supervision and treatment. Mental health providers have an armamentarium of risk assessment methods and structured treatments to reverse the suicide process. Clinicians have an accepted standard of care for assessing and treating suicidal inmates. Good risk management is about good inmate/patient care, which includes a thorough documentation of historical and current information as it relates to suicide stages, M.A.P. modalities, and corresponding treatment interventions and suicide precautions. The therapeutic relationship is the power source for validating an inmate's suicide experience and engaging the inmate to work on reversing the process.

Professional correctional standards exist to guide institutions toward implementing suicide prevention programs that are clinically, ethically, and legally sound. Good prevention programs provide risk screening and assessment, housing, levels of staff supervision, process interventions, administrative reviews, and regular staff training. A number of model programs exist and a good variety of program resources are available to guide an institution toward developing and implementing a solid suicide prevention program. Program outcome research has proven convincingly that such programs are successful, reducing the number of suicides significantly and becoming the major source of legal defense in successfully protecting an institution. Taking short cuts, providing inadequate staffing, and using controversial methods which deviate from the standard suicide prevention program increase the risk for inmate suicide and an institution's liability.

Inmate suicides are traumatic events for staff, inmate peers, and family members. Reaching out to these people through debriefing, survivor counseling, condolences, and family support are all important parts of a suicide prevention program. Such efforts can decrease the risk of suicide for others and reduce the likelihood of a family bringing litigation upon an institution. The general stress associated with correctional work cannot be underestimated, and may very well lead to depression, anxiety, physical illnesses, relationship loss, alcohol abuse, anger, and for some, entry into the suicide process. Executive and department head meetings, officer roll calls, staff recalls, and staff training should openly acknowledge the high risk nature of correctional work and support employee assistance program services to reduce or avert these difficulties. Taking care of staff, each other, and inmates is what the corrections business should be all about.

In closing, the author believes returning to a therapy transcript with a suicidal inmate some seventeen years ago will essentially summarize the process approach to suicide prevention behind bars.

"You asked me my reasons for living, Doc. I ain't got none. My old lady is shacked up with my partner. Never gonna see my kids again. I got 30 more years to do in this fuckin' hole, and I'm tired of all the bullshit. That's all it is, bullshit! Fuck it, who would care if I hung up anyway?" ("Mickey," cited in Bonner 1992a)

Note: The forgoing quote was taken from Chapter 19 of *Isolation, Seclusion, and Psychosocial Vulnerability as Risk Factors for Suicide Behind Bars* by R. L. Bonner (1992) in *Assessment and prediction of suicide* by R. Maris, A. Berman, J. Maltsberger, & R. Yufit (Eds). Copyright by Guilford Press. Used with permission.

No matter our position, no matter how much we know or do not know about suicide, no matter how sophisticated our screening and assessment methods might be, no matter how elaborate and empirically-supported our process interventions might be, no matter how well designed our research studies might be, no matter how well developed and documented our suicide prevention programs might be, no matter how well written our professional standards might be, no matter how well developed our training lesson plans might be, the success of our efforts will simply come down to how we answer Mickey's poignant question, "Who would care if I hung up anyway?"

References

American Correctional Association (2004). *Performance-Based Standards for Adult Local Detention Facilities, 4ᵗʰ Edition.* Lanham, MD: American Correctional Association.

American Correctional Association (1991). *ACA suicide prevention in custody: A mini-correspondence course.* Laurel, MD: American Correctional Association.

Asnis, G., Friedman, R., & Sanderson, W. (1993). Suicidal behavior in adult psychiatric outpatients. *American Journal of Psychiatry,* 150, 1009–1015

Barlow, D. (2004). Psychological treatments. *American Psychologist,* 59(9), 869–878.

Beck, A. T. (1987). *Beck Hopelessness Scale.* San Antonio, TX: The Psychological Corporation.

Beck, A. T., Kovacs, M., & Weissman, A. (1979). Assessment of suicidal intention: The Scale for Suicidal Ideation. *Journal of Consulting and Clinical Psychology,* 47(2), 343–352.

Beck, A. T., Schuyler, D., & Herman, I. (1974). Development of the suicide intent scales. In A. T. Beck & D. J. Lettieri (Eds.), *The prediction of suicide* (pp. 45–56). Bowie, MD: Charles Press.

Beck, A. T., & Steer, R. A. (1987). *Manual for the Revised Beck Depression Inventory.* San Antonio, TX: The Psychological Corporation.

Beck, A. T., Steer, R. A., Beck, J. S., & Newman, C. (1993). Hopelessness, depression, suicide ideation and clinical diagnosis of depression. *Suicide and Life-Threatening Behavior,* 23(2), 139–145.

Beck, A. T., Weissman, A., Lester, D., & Trexler, L. (1974). The measurement of pessimism: The Hopelessness Scale. *Journal of Consulting and Clinical Psychology, 42,* 861–865.

Bongar, B. (2002). *The suicidal patient: Clinical and legal standards* (second edition). Washington, DC: American Psychological Association.

Bonner, R. L. (2006a). Stressful segregation housing and psychosocial vulnerability in prison suicide ideators. *Suicide and Life-Threatening Behavior,* In Press.

Bonner, R. L. (2006b). Managing prisoners with mental health problems and other special needs. In G. Dear (Ed.), *Preventing suicide and other self-harm behavior in prison.* United Kingdom: Palgrave-Macmillian Publisher, In Press.

Bonner, R. L. (2005a). Ethical and professional issues for mental health providers in corrections. In L. VandeCreek & J. Allen (Eds.), *Innovations in clinical practice: Focus on health and wellness.* Sarasota, FL: Professional Resource Exchange.

Bonner, R. L. (2005b). *A psychotherapist's dark journey into the suicidal mind: A relationship approach to understanding and healing.* Lincoln, NE: iUniverse Press.

Bonner, R. L. (2005c). Re-evaluation the use of segregation in corrections. *Corrections Today, 67*(3), 16.

Bonner, R. L. (2005d). Suicide watches by inmates benefit whom? *American Psychological Association Monitor, 36*(7), 8.

Bonner, R. L. (2002). Rethinking suicide prevention and manipulative behavior in corrections. *Jail Suicide/Mental Health Update, 10*(4), 7–9.

Bonner, R. L. (2001). Moving suicide risk assessment into the next millennium: Lessons from our past. In D. Lester (Ed.), *Suicide prevention: Resources for the new millennium* (pp.83–103) Philadelphia, PA: Taylor and Francis.

Bonner, R. L. (2000). Correctional suicide prevention in the year 2000 and beyond. *Suicide and Life-Threatening Behavior, 30*(4), 370–376.

Bonner, R. L. (1998). Management of the mentally ill in custody: A marriage of corrections and mental health care for success. *Jail Suicide/Mental Health Update,* 8(1), 14–15.

Bonner, R. L. (1992a). Isolation, seclusion, and psychosocial vulnerability as risk factors for suicide behind bars. In R. Maris, A. Berman, J. Maltsberger, & R. Yufit (Eds.), *Assessment and prediction of suicide* (pp. 398–420). New York : Guilford.

Bonner, R. L. (1992b). Suicide prevention in correctional facilities. In L. Vande-Creek, S. Knapp, & T. Jackson (Eds.), *Innovations in clinical practice: A source book* (Volume 11) (pp. 467–480). Sarasota, FL: Professional Resource Press

Bonner, R. L. (1990). A M.A.P. to the clinical assessment of suicide risk. *Journal of Mental Health Counseling,* 12(2), 231–236.

Bonner, R. L. (1989). It's time to get back to basics in suicidology: Empathy revisited. *American Association of Suicidology Newslink,* 15(1), 6–7.

Bonner, R. L. & VandeCreek, L. D. (2006). Ethical decision making for correctional mental health providers. *Criminal Justice and Behavior: An International Journal,* In Press.

Bonner, R. L., & Michalik-Bonner, D. (1996). The suicidal patient in private practice: A multimodal approach. *Psychotherapy in Private Practice,* 14(4), 1–15.

Bonner, R. L., & Rich, A. R. (1992). Cognitive vulnerability and hopelessness among correctional inmates: A state of mind model. *Journal of Offender Rehabilitation,* 17(3/4), 113–122.

Bonner, R. L., & Rich, A. R. (1990). Psychosocial vulnerability, life stress, and suicide ideation in a jail population: A cross-validation study. Suicide *and Life-Threatening Behavior,* 20, 213–224.

Clum, G. A., & Febbraro, G. M. (2004) Social problem solving and suicide risk. In E. Chang, T. D'Zurilla, & L. Sanna (Eds.), *Social problem solving: Theory, research, and training* (pp. 67–82). Washington, DC: American Psychological Association.

Cohen, F. (1992). Liability for custodial suicide: the information base requirements. *Jail Suicide/Mental Health Update,* 4(2), 1–11.

Cornelius, G. F. (1994). *Stressed out: Strategies for living and working with stress in corrections.* Laurel, MD: American Correctional Association.

Couturier, L., & Maue, F. M. (2000). Suicide prevention initiatives in a large statewide Department of Corrections: A full-court press to save lives. *Jail Suicide/Mental Health Update,* 9(4), 1–8.

Cox, J., Lansberg, G., & Paravati, M. (1989). The essential components of a crisis intervention program for local jails: The New York local forensic suicide prevention crisis service model. *Psychiatric Quarterly,* 60(2), 103–118.

Crosby, A. E., Cheltenham, B. S., & Sachs, J. J. (1999). Incidence of suicidal ideation and behavior in the United States. *Suicide and Life-Threatening Behavior,* 29(2), 131–140.

Danto, B. (1997). Suicide litigation as an agent of change. *Behavioral Sciences and the Law,* 15(4), 415–425.

Ellis, T., & Newman, C. (1996). *Choosing to live: How to defeat suicide through cognitive therapy.* Oakland, CA: New Harbinger Publications.

Farand, L., Chagnon, F., Renaud, J., & Rivard, M. (2005). Completed suicides among Quebec adolescents involved with juvenile justice and child welfare services. *Suicide and Life-Threatening Behavior,* In Press.

Gunn, J., Robertson, G., Dell, S., & Way, C. (1978). *Psychiatric aspects of imprisonment.* London: Academic Press.

Guttmacher, L. (1994). *Psychopharmacological and electroconvulsive therapy.* Washington, DC: American Psychiatric Association.

Hayes, L. M. (2005a). A practitioner's guide to developing and maintaining a sound suicide prevention policy. *Jail Suicide/Mental Health Update,* 13(4), 1–20.

Hayes, L. M. (2005b). *Personal communications: Revision and Update of the Training Curriculum on Correctional Suicide Prevention.* Mansfield, MA: National Center for Institutions and Alternatives.

Hayes, L. M. (2004a). Special issue: Juvenile suicide in confinement: Findings from the first national study. *Jail Suicide/Mental Health Update,* 13(2), 1–16.

Hayes, L. M. (2004b). State jail standards and suicide prevention: A report card. *Jail Suicide/Mental Health Update,* 13(3), 8–10.

Hayes, L. M. (2003). Use of "no harm" contracts and other controversial issues in suicide prevention. *Jail Suicide/Mental Health Update,* 12(2), 1–9.

Hayes, L. M. (2001). Special issue: Preventing suicide through prompt intervention. *Jail Suicide/Mental Health Update,* 10(3), 1–7.

Hayes, L. M. (1999). Special issue: The uncertain world of jail suicide litigation. *Jail Suicide/Mental Health Update,* 8(4), 1–3.

Hayes, L. M. (1997). No suicide contracts in the correctional environment. *Jail Suicide/Mental Health Update,* 7(2), 7–9.

Hayes, L. M. (1995a). *Prison suicide: An overview and guide to prevention.* Mansfield, MA: National Center for Institutions and Alternatives.

Hayes, L. M. (1995b). Use of inmates to conduct suicide watch and other controversial issues in suicide prevention. *Jail Suicide/Mental Health Update,* 6(1), 1–6.

Hayes, L. M. (1992). Critical incident stress: Responding to jail staff as victims. *Jail Suicide/Mental Health Update,* 4(3), 10–11.

Hayes, L. M., & Kajdin, B. (1981). And darkness closes in: National study of jail suicides. Washington, DC: National Center for Institutions and Alternatives.

Hayes, L. M., & Rowan, J. R. (1988). National study of jail suicides. Alexandria, VA: National Center for Institutions and Alternatives.

He, X., Felthous, M., Holzer, C., Nathan, M., & Veasey, S. (2001). Factors in prison suicides: One year study in Texas. *Journal of Forensic Sciences,* 46(4), 896–901.

Hoyer, D. L., Smith, B. L., Murphy, S. L., & Kochanet, M. A. (2001). Deaths: Final data for national vital statistics, 49. Hyattsville, MD: National Center for Health Statistics.

Jobes, D. A., & Bermna, A. L. (1993). Suicide and malpractice liability: Assessing and revising policies, procedures, and practice of outpatient settings. *Professional Psychology: Research and Practice, 24*, 91–99.

Lazarus, A. (1995). Multimodal therapy. In R. J. Corsini & D. Wedding (Eds.), *Current psychotherapies, 5th edition* (pp. 322–355). Itasca, IL: Peacock.

Lazarus, A. (1989). *The practice of multimodal therapy.* Baltimore, Maryland: John Hopkins University Press.

Lee, D. W. (2002). Personal liability against correctional officials and employees for failure to protect the suicidal inmate under 42 USC 1983. *Jail Suicide/ Mental Health Update, 11*(1), 1–8.

Lester, D., & Danto, B. L. (1993). *Suicide behind bars: Prediction and prevention.* Philadelphia, PA: The Charles Press.

Linn-Gust, M. (2004). When suicide hits home…again. *Surviving Suicide, 16*(4), 4–5.

Linehan, M. (1999). Standard protocol for assessing and treating suicidal behaviors for patients in treatment. In D. Jacobs (Ed.), *The Harvard medical guide to suicide assessment and intervention* (pp. 146–187). San Francisco, CA: Jossey Bass Publishers.

Linehan, M. M. (1987). Dialectical behavior therapy for borderline personality disorder. *Bulletin of the Menninger Clinic, 51*, 261–276.

Linehan, M. (1985). Reasons for living inventory. In P. A. Keller & L. G. Ritt (Eds.), *Innovations in clinical practice* (vol.4, pp. 321–330). Sarasota, FL: Professional Resource Exchange.

Loo, R. (2003). A meta-analysis of police suicide: Findings and issues. *Suicide and Life-Threatening Behavior, 33*(3), 313–325.

Maruschak, L. (2004). HIV in prisons and jails, 2002. U.S. Department of Justice. *Bureau of Justice Statistics Bulletin,* 1–12.

Metzner, J. L., Cohen, F., Grossman, L. S., & Wettstein, R. M. (1998). Treatment in jails and prisons. In R. M. Wettstein (Ed.), *Treatment of offenders with mental disorders.* New York, NY: Guilford.

National Commission on Correctional Health Care. (2003). 2003 Standards for Health Services in Prisons. Chicago, IL: National Commission on Correctional Health Care.

O'Leary, W. D. (1989). Custodial suicide: Evolving liability in corrections. *Psychiatric Quarterly, 60,* 31–71.

Orbach, I., Mikulciner, M., Gilboa-Schectman, E., & Sirota, P. (2003). Mental pain and its relationship to suicidality and life meaning. *Suicide and Life-Threatening Behavior, 33*(3), 242–248.

Quinnett, P. (1997). *Suicide: The forever decision.* New York, New York: The Crossroad Publishing Company.

Reynolds, W. M. (1987). Suicidal Ideation Questionnaires. Odesa, FL: Psychological Assessment Resources.

Rich, A. R., & Bonner, R. L. (2004). Mediators and moderators of social problem solving. In E. Chang, T. D'Zurilla, & L. Sanna (Eds.), *Social problem solving: Theory, research, and training* (pp. 29–45). Washington, DC: American Psychological Association.

Robertson, J. E. (2004). The impact of Farmer v. Brennan on jailers' personal liability for custodial suicides: Ten years later. *Jail Suicide/Mental Health Update, 13*(1), 1–6.

Robertson, A., & Husain, J. (2001). Prevalence of mental illness and substance abuse disorders among incarcerated juvenile offenders. Jackson, MS: Mississippi Department of Public Safety and Department of Health.

Rowan, J. R., & Hayes, L. M. (1988). *Training curriculum on suicide detection and prevention in jails and lock-ups.* Washington, DC: National Center for Institutions and Alternatives.

Roy, A. (1991). Psychiatric treatment in suicide prevention. In D. Lester (Ed.), *Suicide prevention: Resources for the millennium* (pp. 103–127). Philadelphia, PA: Taylor and Francis.

Rudd, M. D., Joiner, T., & Rajab, M. H. (2001). *Treating suicidal behavior: An effective, time-limited approach.* New York: Guilford.

Salive, M. E., Gordon, S., & Brewer, T. (1989). Suicide mortality in the Maryland State Prison System 1979–1987. *Journal of the American Medical Association,* 262(3), 365–369.

Salzman, C. (1999). Treatment of the suicidal patient with psychotropic drugs and ECT. In D. Jacobs (Ed.), *The Harvard medical guide to suicide assessment and intervention* (pp. 372–382). San Francisco, CA: Jossey Bass Publishers.

Sanchez, H. G. (1999). Inmate suicide and the psychological autopsy process. *Jail Suicide/Mental Health Update,* 8(3), 3–9.

Shneidman, E. (2004). *Autopsy of a suicidal mind.* New York, New York: The Oxford Press.

Shneidman, E. (2001). *Comprehending suicide.* Washington, DC: American Psychological Association.

Shneidman, E. (1999). The psychological pain assessment scale. *Suicide and Life-Threatening Behavior,* 29, 287–294.

Snyder, H. N. (2005). Is suicide more common inside or outside juvenile facilities? *Corrections Today* (February 2005), 84–88.

Sovronsky, H. R., & Shapiro, I. (1989). The New York State model suicide prevention training program for local correctional officers. *Psychiatric Quarterly,* 60(2), 139–150.

Spellman, A., & Heyne, B. (1989). Suicide? accident? predictable? avoidable? The psychological autopsy in jail suicides. *Psychiatric Quarterly,* 60(2), 173–184.

Tanney, B. L. (1992). Mental disorders, psychiatric patients, and suicide. In R. Maris, A. Berman, J. Maltsberger, & R. Yufit (Eds.), *Assessment and prediction of suicide* (pp. 277–320. New York: Guilford.

Toch, H. (1992). *Mosaic of despair: Human breakdown in prison.* Washington, DC: American Psychological Association.

Toch, H., & Grant, J. D. (2005). *Police as problem solvers*. Washington, DC: American Psychological Association.

Van Pragg, H. (1991). Suicide and aggression: Are they biologically two sides of the same coin. In D. Lester (Ed.), *Suicide prevention: Resources for the millennium* (pp. 45–64). Philadelphia, PA Taylor and Francis.

White, T. W., & Schimmel, D. J. (1995). Suicide prevention in federal prisons: A successful five-step program. In L. Hayes (Ed.), *Prison suicide: An overview and guide to prevention* (pp. 46–57). Mansfield, MA: National Center for Institutions and Alternatives.

About the Author

Ronald L. Bonner, Psy.D., is a clinical psychologist who has worked with offenders for the last nineteen years. During this period, he has worked in a jail inpatient crisis stabilization unit, a maximum-security penitentiary, two medium-security correctional institutions, and private practice. His research interests include clinical suicidology, depression, and ethical decision-making in correctional mental health care. Dr. Bonner has presented his research to numerous professional meetings and has authored or co-authored more than fifty publications. He has served as a consulting editor for *Suicide and Life-Threatening Behavior* for the last fifteen years and is also currently a member of the Ethics Hotline Workgroup for the American Association for Correctional and Forensic Psychology. Dr. Bonner lives in the country with his wife, Diane, a child clinical psychologist; his two rowdy sons, Jason and Joshua; his attention-seeking dog, "Bandit"; and his projective feline, "Rorschach."

The views expressed in this work are solely those of the author and do not necessarily represent his institutional or organization affiliations. He may be contacted at Three South Market Street, Selinsgrove, PA 17870, (570) 374-4305 (e-mail-rbonner@bop.gov).

978-0-595-36982-9
0-595-36982-0

www.ingramcontent.com/pod-product-compliance
Lightning Source LLC
Chambersburg PA
CBHW030405290526
45785CB00004B/1907